GOLDENBRIDGE

A VIEW FROM VALPARAISO

VERITAS

TERESITA DURKAN

GOLDENBRIDGE

A VIEW FROM VALPARAISO

VERITAS

First published 1997 by
Veritas Publications
7/8 Lower Abbey Street
Dublin 1

Copyright © Teresita Durkan 1997

ISBN 1 85390 303 5

British Library Cataloguing
in Publication Data.
A catalogue record for
this book is available
from the British Library.

Cover photography by Bill Doyle
Cover design by Bill Bolger
Printed in the Republic of Ireland by Betaprint Ltd, Dublin

For children who suffer
and those who try to love and
help them

CONTENTS

INTRODUCTION

In February 1996, Radio Telefís Eireann broadcast a programme which attracted widespread public attention: in telling the story of a daughter's search for the mother who had never acknowledged her, it depicted children in Goldenbridge Industrial School in west Dublin four decades ago, as having painful memories of the time they spent in public care there.

The programme touched a sore spot in the conscience of the Irish people. And, by a kind of collective rush to judgment, the word Goldenbridge quickly became associated with all that was flawed and wanting in the country's provision for the children who had been in its residential care over many generations.

News of the television programme reached me in Valparaiso where I have lived since 1989. It came as no surprise to me that sad personal experiences - which were almost inevitable under a national child-care system that was poor, penny-pinching, understaffed, socially-condescending and dismally provided for - should become the focus of public concern. What did surprise me was that adverse judgment should have been passed, so very quickly, on the place known as Goldenbridge.

I had worked in Irish education for more than thirty years, five of the most formative and personally-challenging of them in schools in Goldenbridge. That was from 1959 to 1964, part of the period covered by the television docu-drama. I had a different memory of the place and what it stood for, from the image created in the public mind as a result of the television programme.

I decided that I must look critically again at the

Goldenbridge I knew during those years, and try to hold in steady focus a place that had a lasting influence on my own life. For Goldenbridge was, in a very real way, the starting-point of a journey that has led me to share whatever I have now with poor children in less fortunate parts of the world.

So this book is a personal memoir. I leave it to others to evaluate, in a more searching and socially-objective way, the contribution that Goldenbridge made to the education of the children and the lives of struggling families in west Dublin for almost 150 years.

Teresita Durkan

PART 1

They are begging us, you see, in their wordless way
To do something, to speak on their behalf...
Derek Mahon: 'In a Disused Shed in Wexford'.

ALONG THE CANAL

There are two cemeteries in Goldenbridge on the banks of the Grand Canal where it marks the southern boundary of Inchicore. The larger of the two, a small burial-ground as city cemeteries go and no longer in use, is known locally as the DOM from the lettering over the gate. If you ask some of the youngsters playing along the street what DOM means they'll probably shrug their shoulders or laugh and say 'dead old men.'

But the DOM in its early days was a source of pride and satisfaction to the people of west Dublin, that is in so far as a cemetery can ever be entirely a cause of satisfaction. It was the first separate burial-ground for Catholics to be legally sanctioned in the capital after the era of the Penal Laws. No longer obliged to find their last resting-place in what they looked on as alien or unconsecrated ground - or be subjected to the indignity of lying forever in Bully's Acre - the Catholics of west Dublin were pleased to be allowed to lay their dead to rest in the DOM on the north bank of the Grand Canal in Goldenbridge.

There, among the yews and long grasses and tilting monuments, you'll find the weather-worn tombstones of Queen's Counsellors, doctors, apothecaries, merchants, businessmen, Land Registry employees, and one whose inscription stays in my mind because he's described on his tombstone as 'A Member of the Paving Board'.

They sleep now between the site of the former Richmond Military Barracks - today Saint Michael's Housing Estate - and the canal. Like the Pharaohs of old, though with less public advertence, they're sometimes surrounded by concealed treasures, the loot from some local heist, supplies for a cider-party, gear for sniffing glue or for ingesting or supplying other illegal substances, or just stuff that 'fell off a lorry'.

But the DOM is mostly a peaceful place today, a small enclave of the dead, gradually taking on the appearance of a little park with dark tree-crowns and birdsong and flights of pigeons. It belongs to a closed, almost-forgotten chapter in the history of post-Catholic Emancipation Dublin.

The other Goldenbridge cemetery is even smaller. Located a few hundred yards further west along the same bank of the Grand Canal, it represents a mute chapter from that period of Irish history too, a fragment from a fading epoch. Not quite a closed book yet, but nearing its last pages, I think.

This cemetery contains a more distilled or maybe rarefied selection of the Irish population of that same post-Catholic Emancipation era – the period that stretched, broadly speaking, from the prime of Daniel O'Connell to the decline of Eamon De Valera. It is the community cemetery of the Dublin Sisters of Mercy.

Located at the far end of the convent grounds in Goldenbridge, this tiny patch of earth is the last resting-place of several hundreds of women whom their society and Church – Irish society and the Irish Catholic Church – encouraged to accept one of the most self-denying roles in the struggle for the development of their impoverished country in the nineteenth and early twentieth centuries.

They were to renounce marriage, live sparingly in ascetical communities, and devote their incomes and energies – and the pooled capital they generated in that way – to alleviating poverty. They were to help provide the basic educational, social and health services that the state was as yet unable or unwilling to offer to its hundreds of thousands of poor and destitute citizens. And when the disaster of the Great Famine struck in the mid-nineteenth century many of them followed the Irish diaspora to the countries that received the fleeing emigrants.

They were there, too, for succeeding waves of Irish men and women whom poverty drove out in search of a living during the century that followed. They were to be found working in large and small communities in places as far apart as Auckland and Buenos Aires, San Francisco and Johannesburg.

Those who stayed on to work in Dublin sleep now in the shadow of the yews in Goldenbridge. They lie under much more modest funerary monuments than the solid citizens down the road in the DOM, from whose families many of them came. If you walk around their little cemetery today, its tiny tablet grave-markers may strike you as flat, uniform and self-effacing to a point hardly worthy of women who made such an important contribution to the development of Irish society in their era. But they lived by beliefs and aspirations that didn't set store by sculpted monuments, at least for themselves. They came out of - and their sparse lives clearly expressed - something that was striving and ascetic in the ethos of an Ireland that had been struggling for centuries against a crippling poverty. If they aspired to any riches they would have thought of these as riches of the spirit, and they would have looked for their models to a distant Irish monastic past, or to some more recent European era of religious devotion and charity. But such pasts, however devoutly they might be invoked, didn't guarantee a life-giving and personally-fulfiling present for everyone who tried to emulate them, and many of these women suffered for it.

Their achievement was that they fought, with real effect, against the poverty of a poor people in poor times. Their suffering was that they themselves became, in certain ways, locked into the same narrow grid of deprivation with those they helped, hostages to the rigid and limiting social vision that held sway across a large and needy part of Irish society during those difficult decades. Poverty, even when voluntarily accepted, is a harsh and often a hardening condition. It is also a dispiriting and sometimes a demeaning one.

I remember hearing one of these women say, 'If you can't realise the ideal, then you must idealise the real.' It was a palliative and self-defeating philosophy at best, and it was particularly inappropriate in the Ireland of the mid-twentieth century. And yet this was a generous, hard-working woman, trying to make a little peace with the otherwise unendurable conditions in which she found herself at work.

The more actively these women tried to help their less-fortunate neighbours to rise from the trough of poverty that sucked down so much of the energy of Irish life - before the tide began to turn slowly against poverty in the second half of the twentieth century - the easier it was for the limitations of such a hard life to colonise their own souls and restrict in various ways their sensibility and vision. And yet very few sections of Irish society worked with more dedication, or were as unsparing of themselves and their resources for the benefit of their needier fellow-citizens throughout those long and difficult years.

I have sometimes watched a flight of doves rise from the direction of one of the Goldenbridge cemeteries on a sunny day. When the light catches their plumage there are sudden flashes of a pure, ephemeral white. The birds look free, graceful, airborne. But when they circle and descend to earth again they lose that brightness and become flapping, dumpy, motley-hued pigeons.

The women who lie in the Goldenbridge Mercy cemetery seem to me to have been a bit like that. They came in different shapes and sizes. They could shine with great beauty sometimes, but they could show opaque enough at other moments. For myself, I think I can speak of them with a kind of privileged intimacy. To borrow a phrase from Yeats, 'they were my chosen comrades many a year, a portion of my mind and life, as it were'. And although I shall not lie among them in death, I am glad to have shared their ideals and efforts to overcome poverty in Ireland during some of the most active years of my life.

GETTING THERE

I arrived in Goldenbridge on 20 May 1959. All my possessions that morning were either on my back or packed tightly into a brown cardboard suitcase which also contained my primary-teacher's certificate.

When I arrived in Chile thirty years later, almost to the day, I had two suitcases, two boxes of books, a handful of traveller's cheques along with the passport in my body-belt. In my luggage there was a letter from the Irish Department of Education telling me the amount I was entitled to by way of an early-retirement pension.

I hadn't much to show on the material level for my thirty years of work in Irish education, but I was content to have it that way. It was the life I had chosen. I had no real regrets about the three decades I had spent in the Sisters of Mercy either. Diverging views don't amount to personal regrets. The world has a right to be different from the way you think it ought to be. I had led a reasonably useful and not at all uneventful life, and now I had another one starting.

But I was leaving at this point - leaving Ireland and community life among the Sisters of Mercy. My small craft had been headed towards different waters for some time. The year was 1989.

I was twenty-two years, four months and ten days, and only recently launched on the experience of living in a religious community, when I arrived in Goldenbridge that other May morning thirty years earlier. I had had a short pep-talk from the mistress of novices before I left the centre-house in Carysfort. 'Peace, but not peace at all costs,' she summed up. And I wondered if she had some special reason for telling me that because I was going to Goldenbridge or if it was a bit of good advice she gave to all her novices leaving for their first assignment.

James, the Carysfort groundsman who doubled as a chauffeur for the community car, sat silently behind the wheel of the black Ford, much as he had done all those mornings and evenings when he'd been shuttling us to and fro in a minibus between the novitiate in Carysfort and the community's new primary school on the other side of the city in Coolock. It was hard to know what James was thinking. I'd only had one conversation with him during my three years in Carysfort, and that was about flowers.

But he did remark this morning, as we turned off the main road at Emmet House in Inchicore and headed up Saint Vincent's Street in the direction of the canal, that the landmark for nearly every Convent of Mercy in the country was some well-known pub. I wasn't sure what he was signalling by that. I wanted to tell him that although there were eleven pubs in Louisburgh when I was small, none of them was what you might call a signpost for the Convent of Mercy.

About three-quarters of the way up the dead-end street that looked as if it led straight into the canal, we turned right and drove in through the high gates of the convent. On the far side of the road a bit further on was the entrance to the old cemetery called the DOM.

'It's certainly different from Carysfort Park,' I thought when I took my first searching look at it. The convent and its surrounding buildings were old, but not with the period elegance of Carysfort. No pillared Georgian mansion on rising ground here, no gabled red-brick Victorian training college, no long, curving avenue. This was just a set of scattered old buildings strung out along the periphery of some bare and smallish convent grounds. To my eyes that morning most of them looked grey and worn and vaguely hand-me-down.

Goldenbridge, I had been told by Carmel who knew the

place before I did, had started life in the 1850s as an industrial school, a female convict-refuge and a laundry. She leaned on the word 'convict-refuge', and said I'd probably feel at home there. I said, 'Hm,' and deferred further comment. She told me that Goldenbridge also had the reputation of having stayed closer to the needs of poor and destitute people, over the course of its 103 active years, than almost any of the other Dublin convents. In the 1950s that was saying something.

The superior was at the door to welcome us. A small, purplish-faced woman in her late sixties, with prominent eyes and an inquiring bird-like smile. She had the gait of a person who took herself seriously. She was called Virgilius, but of course she also had a nickname. A relative of hers worked in the Town Planning section of Dublin Corporation, a man whom she used to quote occasionally as an expert on matters of building. So the principal of the school, who was no particular admirer of hers, called her the Town Planner, and the name stuck.

It wasn't a bad name. She was an expert on drains, pipes, man-holes, sewerage, broken slates, weeds, boundary walls and innumerable details of household hygiene. She expended great thought on how to make shrewd household economies, and she had an unparalleled devotion to the keeping of accurate convent accounts.

She turned out, as time went on, to be a decent enough sort, a woman with her kindly sides, fond of making little verbal sallies that she thought of as witty. But she was fussy and pernickety and very literal-minded about many things. Afterwards I'd come to think that she missed the birdsong – and probably the sweep of the woods too – from measuring too closely the branches of the next tree she was about to prune. But then there weren't many trees in Goldenbridge in the 1950s.

Her legacy to the place, apart from a lifetime spent teaching efficiently in its schools, would be three sets of squat concrete toilet buildings, one for each of the main school buildings. God knows they were badly needed.

I arrived shortly before lunchtime so she called 'one of the juniors' – a favourite phrase of hers – to show me around. The junior turned out to be a Donegal woman a few years older than myself. Unlike me – who had just recently arrived at the lowly grade of black novice – Peter was a full member of the community, one of the 'finally professed'. The difference seemed to be important. She mentioned the word 'seniority' a few times as we walked around. And like those other weighty words from our novitiate – 'perfection' and 'worldliness', the one being good, and the other very bad – seniority seemed to be a big deal.

I was to get to know Peter well over the next few years as we worked side by side in school and travelled in and out to Earlsfort Terrace as night students at the university, and we were to reach a good working agreement about most things. The differences between us I'd put down to her being a small, quick Donegal woman with the certainties of maths and commerce, which she was teaching, etched sharply across her mental landscape, while I was still an amorphous, gangling Mayo girl with history and poetry and a chronic impressionablity creating shifting shapes on mine.

And yet I was to learn some real history from Peter. It was from her, I think, that I got my first intimations that Ireland in the 1950s was not in all respects the peaceful place I had assumed it to be. She had met the B Specials.

Born in a county that shared a stretch of the border with Northern Ireland, she told me what it was like to wonder if your neighbour mightn't be, secretly, a collaborator with the special border forces. She also told me about acquaintances being stopped and harassed by B Special patrols at night on their way home from shopping in Strabane.

I listened, but without real understanding, I think. It would be a full ten years later – when the Troubles had erupted publicly again in Northern Ireland in 1969 and the abolition of the Border Special Force was one of the first urgent issues - before I'd realise how little I knew about the fraught history and bitter divisions still persisting in another part of my own country.

'That's Keogh Square, over there,' she pointed to a complex of dark-grey buildings just opposite the convent gate. They dominated the skyline and filled the entire block beside the DOM on the other side of the road.

'You'll have heard of it, I suppose?'

I had, but she gave me a brief run-through of its recent history, anyway.

'It used to be Richmond Barracks, a garrison headquarters in the days of the British, but it belongs to the Dublin Corporation Housing Department now. And it's a real black hole, if ever there was one. The most run-down set of flats in the whole of the city, more like shelter than housing. I pity the poor people who have to try and bring up their children there...'

She broke off and pursed her lips tightly in disapproval.

'But you'll get to know what it's like over there soon enough.'

She turned and walked back towards the convent. I followed her in through the front door.

And on my hill in Valparaiso now, thirty-seven years later, I realise how unconsciously prophetic her words were. The day would come when I'd actually go to live 'over there', and it would prove to be one of the most revealing and useful experiences of my life. One of my most cherished friendships would blossom there, and I'd find the courage to face alone into the next - the Chilean - phase of my life.

But in May 1959 all that lay in the unknown future. It was to happen in a different epoch of the history of the flats, and at a much later period of my own life.

A BLACK NOVICE

Picture me then, aged twenty-two, arriving in Goldenbridge on a sunny May morning in 1959. I had spent the five years before that in Carysfort. From 1954 to 1956, I was a student in the training college, preparing to be a primary teacher. The next three years I spent as a postulant and novice in the centre-house of the Dublin Sisters of Mercy, located in the same grounds. I had taught for a few months in national schools in Blackrock and Coolock, but Goldenbridge was my first real assignment. I was in every way a fresh sprout from the enclosed garden of the novitiate.

'My dear green sisters,' a Jesuit retreat-master had addressed us during our novices' retreat the previous summer. He was an eloquent, cultured, well-travelled man, a prominent member of the Arts Council of Ireland. He should know.

The day was warm, but I was wearing the regulation dress, an all-weather black Mercy habit. The long serge skirt reached almost to my toes, pleated, belted and bulging with the thickness of the heavy woollen petticoat I was wearing underneath. I had a black pocket tied around my waist over the petticoat, and a pin-cushion dangling from that on a black cord.

The pin-cushion was called a boss. I remember that, because it fell off one day when I was getting out of the No. 20 bus in Harcourt Street on the way to the university. The conductor picked it up and handed it back to me.

'You dropped your... thing,' he said politely.

I wanted to tell him it was called a boss or a pincushion, but I was too embarrassed to say anything except 'thanks'.

Our headgear was fairly complicated too. White starched linen assembled with the help of pins from four different pieces that had to be laundered separately; coif, guimp, dimity and domino. Over that there was a carefully-pleated black veil. We had been taught to say a prayer over each of these items while we were dressing in the morning, but I had never been able to manage it.

A pair of wide, detachable over-sleeves, a dangling leather belt called a cincture, an outsize rosary beads with a brass crucifix, and a black-and-white Mercy cross stuck in the knot of the cincture, made up the rest of the habit. And there was a woollen shawl in case the day turned cold.

Whether it was the dress of a medieval abbess or an eighteenth-century widow, I couldn't say. The odd thing was I didn't find it very strange at the time. It was different certainly, but I'd been looking at it almost every day since I started going to school at the age of four.

It was uncomfortable to work in, though, and unhygienic in hot weather, and to send it out for dry-cleaning was unknown. During the holidays we had to rip it out, make it over, and sew it back together again, pleat by pleat, when a panel of not-so-worn serge was supplied by the bursar to replace the frayed parts.

So the only way you could identify any of us, individually, back then, was by looking at the face framed in white starch, visible from eyebrows to chin only. It was just as well you couldn't see our poor, shorn, semi-bald heads. Some great ecclesiastical guru must have decreed that, being monks *manqués*, the likes of us ought to be kept next-best-thing to tonsured.

'That's part of the original convent building,' Peter pointed to the corridor leading right from the front door. 'And that's the community room... and this bit was added on in the late 1920s – we call it Connolly Avenue...'

She was a thorough guide. She even made sure to show me, in passing, where to pick up the community alarm-clock and how to ring the house-bell when my turn came to give the call some morning at 5.30. I tried not to show how bewildered I felt.

The oldest part of the convent was a gabled red-brick building with a small neo-Gothic chapel as its main feature. It was probably imposing in a modest way when it was first built there in open country near the bank of the Grand Canal during the decade immediately after the Great Famine – another testimony to the gathering impetus of Catholic revival in the years following Emancipation.

But various extensions had been added to it since then. They were piecemeal constructions, tacked on in an economical and *ad hoc* way over the years to make room for the expanding activities of the community. Most of them didn't match the original, nor did they seem to match each other.

The ugliest one was a pillared grey lean-to called a cloister. It ran left from the red-brick area at the front entrance to the convent and extended as far as the garden gate. It was intended as a place where the sisters could pray and take exercise – which meant walking – when the weather was wet. But it was ugly, wind-swept, damp and generally useless. I think the poor men who came to the door used it for shelter and other necessities of nature. It had to be demolished in the 1960s.

The red-brick of the convent – not yet painted the peeling grey that would be the legacy of the Town Planner's successor – had a mellow look about it that first day. Later I'd notice that the brick was poor and porous. All the other buildings, which formed a kind of gapped cordon around the periphery of the grounds, were of grey concrete. They looked dark, rain-washed and old, even on that clear May morning. The big primary school, Peter told me, had over a thousand pupils on its rolls. These were housed in a scattered collection of buildings inconveniently distant from each other and from the outdoor toilets on a wet day. One of them had been a chapel in the days of the military barracks. Its windows were small, narrow, pointed and located high up near the ceiling. This was the Infant Boys' School.

A forthright Mayo woman called Athanasius, who was later to undertake some part of my education in the virtue of humility, was teaching there. The only thing that resigned her to working in such a place, she said, was that it was to some extent proof against the principal's prying eyes and ears.

The newest of the school buildings – the one where I was assigned to teach during my first year – dated from the early 1930s. It was the only building on the compound that showed any trace of conventional school architecture. But it had a problem. It was sinking, fast and sideways, into the low, marshy ground along the boundary wall.

The story went that the superior who had built it was so 'near herself' – or possibly so afraid of looking for extra money from the centre-house in Carysfort – that she failed to put in the structural reinforcements necessary to secure the foundations. This building too had to be demolished within a few decades.

I had forgotten about that sinking school – and the crack in the floor of my classroom there – for many years. But it shot back into my mind suddenly one day in Chile. It was 3 March 1985 when, on my first visit to the country during sabbatical leave from Carysfort, I found myself standing on a cracked and slanting floor after the first earthquake I had the misfortune to experience in South America.

During my first three years in Goldenbridge I was what was known as a black novice. It was a lowly rank, like a one-star private in the army, and you reached it by the following route.

First came six months as a postulant in Carysfort. This was to give the community time to decide if you 'suited the life'. Never mind whether the life suited you. It generally didn't at that point, if you told yourself the whole truth. But you hung on for a variety of reasons.

First, it took real guts to turn back when you had set out to follow your vocation in a religious community in Ireland in those years – such was the transcendental aura and the ascription of a virtually immutable social role that had been built up around the venture. Then, the fact that you found it hard was supposed to be an argument in favour of your having a really 'solid ' vocation... and *amour propre* wasn't going to let you fall at the first hurdle. Besides, the odds were that things would get better as you went along, especially when you became a fully-fledged member of the community, one of the 'finally-professed'. But it would take you six years to get to that desired state.

When your time of probation as a postulant was over you were either sent home, or given the white veil and received into the community. There was a special ceremony for the giving of the veil. The choir sang a reiterative Latin chant which would echo in your mind for a long time afterwards:

Elegi abjecta esse in domum Domini mei Jesu Christi.

I have chosen to be an abject in the house of the Lord. 'Abject' or 'object', you might ask yourself later and wryly conclude that, on balance, it came to about the same thing. You weren't a black novice yet, though. For the next two years you were still a white one. It went by the colour of the veil.

Spiritual year came immediately after the reception of the veil. It was the most important rung on the novitiate ladder and the core period of initial religious formation – a strictly-cloistered time of prayer, house-chores, lectures and spiritual reading, punctuated by novitiate classes in which we studied the writings of a curious old Spaniard called Rodriguez. We weren't much into put-down phrases back then – television hadn't yet arrived in Ireland, and the religious life was meant to be a very solemn business – but even to our naive and aspiring minds Rodriguez seemed to most of us to be 'for the birds'.

What we didn't realise was the function he served in inducting us into the system of vowed obedience, the cement that held religious communities together and kept them efficient in their practical functioning. He was the one who introduced us to that celebrated model of religious virtue, the novice who planted cabbages upside down because his superior told him that was the way to do it.

That was blind obedience. That was the height of virtue, or the depth of it, depending on your way of looking at things. You either took it neat, or you swallowed it with a grain of salt. Either way you were likely to be planting little seeds of conflict for yourself, small shoots of double-thinking that could come up to complicate your handling of more complex issues further along the way. But back then in the novitiate during spiritual year it all seemed like harmless, antiquated theory.

After two years as a white novice you were eligible to receive the black veil and make first vows. These were temporary, a set of promises that bound you for three years during which time you were known as a black novice

On 9 May 1959, fifteen of us – an unusually big number even for those times of burgeoning vocations in convents, monasteries and diocesan seminaries – made our first vows in the big chapel in Carysfort. We promised to practise poverty, chastity and obedience, and to serve the poor, sick, and ignorant as Sisters of Mercy for three years. At the end of that time we would come back and ratify the commitment for life.

Ten days after making temporary vows I was assigned to Goldenbridge. It had the reputation of being a hard old station.

THE TERRITORY

The only place I really liked during my guided tour with Peter that first day was the little orchard and garden at the back of the convent. There were neatly laid out drills of vegetables, a couple of glasshouses with flowers and tomatoes, a tiny lawn neatly trimmed, garden seats, and old apple trees in May blossom. It looked homely and inviting, a place where I could – and did – spend pleasant hours.

Over the wall from the greenhouse, following Peter's pointing finger, I got my first glimpse of the secondary school. She was teaching there, she told me. I didn't think it looked any way inviting. Known as 'The Seniors' – because it was in reality the upper part of the primary school and was staffed by selected national teachers – it provided free second-level schooling for youngsters from different parts of west and central Dublin. Free secondary education was not to become available to all Irish children as a provision of the state until seven years later. I was to work in 'The Seniors' for four years, from 1960 to 1964.

But it was another of those poor, hand-me-down buildings that so many Irish schools had to make do with in the 1950s. There was no scheme of state grants for building or extending secondary schools yet, so this one occupied the site – some said the very buildings – that had served as an industrial school and laundry at the end of the previous century.

Its entrance wasn't impressive either. A narrow door in a grey, spike-topped wall led in from the cul-de-sac of tiny houses known as Tram Terrace. On one side were the sprawling junkyards where Toft's Amusements kept their trucks, broken-down equipment and rusty repair sheds. On the other, a tract of waste ground sloped down to a weedy river-bank and a practically invisible little river. This patch of ground hosted a succession of squatters.

One of the them was an old lady who kept a pair of goats. The animals roamed around, most of the time untethered, and they liked to wander out occasionally to meet the scholars. Once in a while they'd send somebody on a sudden and spectacular home-run. I had the experience myself – heart thumping, long skirts flying, veil lifting like a sail in a sudden squall, and a delighted audience cheering me from the windows until I made it to the safety of the back door.

At the far end of the orchard was the little community cemetery. It was a small, high-walled enclosure complete with yew trees and a tiny funerary chapel. I was to stand there many a cold morning with a damp wind blowing in from the canal, trying to keep candles alight, waiting for a funeral to arrive from the Mater or Jervis Street or one of the other communities.

I was to walk the paths of that cemetery many times too, especially when I felt the heavy hand of the principal leaning on me, unjustly as I thought. On days like that I'd look at the little graves, shake my head and say, 'It's alright for you in there.'

Finally, flanking the cemetery, but standing apart with its back to the canal at some distance from the convent, was the industrial school. It was a plain grey rectangular building situated in small grounds of its own. It had a walled yard on one side and an open green area with children's swings in front.

I didn't see the inside of the industrial school that day. In fact, during my five years in Goldenbridge I was relatively seldom to see the inside of the building. This wasn't altogether my own fault. The rules were strict. Cobbler stick to your last, or, more bluntly, mind your own business and don't go poking your nose in where you're not assigned to work. I took the injunction seriously – maybe because it suited me to. An orphanage was the hardest place you could be assigned to work, and I wasn't inclined to tempt fate.

Now, many years later, when I hear someone talking - or when I talk myself - about the 'two worlds', north and south, the two Chiles, the two Santiagos, the two Dublins, the worlds of the haves and have-nots, the domains of the well-off and the poor, I find myself uncomfortable.

Looking back, I know that it's possible to live within the same small world – a community, a convent, a work-compound, a neighbourhood, even a very poor hill in Valparaiso – and to settle for the invisible boundaries that separate such places. I have, in my time, avoided what made me uncomfortable, especially the things that brought me face-to-face with my own passivity and inadequacy.

And, being young in 1959, I was glad that I didn't have to work in the orphanage in Goldenbridge, that I didn't have to mind the hundred or more children who lived there all day every day. I was glad somebody else did it. I'd have been annoyed if anybody back then had called me a coward, but I suppose that's what I was. I was relieved when the shake of the dice landed me on a different work-number.

But one thing I did understand then and have never forgotten. The work that others – often less well-trained and less well-equipped than I was – the kind of work they rose to face every morning was surely of the sort that called for the wisdom and courtesy of the old American-Indian proverb: Never judge a brave until you have walked three moons in his moccasins. Some women walked in those moccasins that I dreaded, all their active lives.

At the beginning it didn't look as if I had really landed on a luckier number, though. The first job I got was minding – the principal said teaching – Sister Kevin's class of sixty-five Infants while she was recovering from surgery in the Mater Hospital.

Kevin was nearing seventy at the time but she was a supernumerary member of the school staff, which meant that she could teach – or be asked to teach – until she dropped. She was a gruff, kindly, independent, chatty woman who had her own erratic views about most things in life. She believed, for example, that every bad turn the weather took in the early 1960s – and we weren't short of them – was caused by 'one of them Russian Sputniks'. She had an unconcealed impatience with the whole tribe of superiors, councillors, school principals and wielders of local or central community authority.

Naturally the school principal – she with the penchant for putting nicknames on people – didn't like to see the junior sisters hanging about with Kevin. I was to develop a lasting affection for her.

For one thing she gave me her copy of *The Irish Times* every day. It was twenty-four hours old by then because she got it after school from a teacher who worked down the corridor from her. She read it in bed, and in due course so did I. It was still regarded as a Protestant paper, and reading it as being a bit above yourself. Kevin also gave me good advice – acquired in the hard school of experience, she assured me – about how to handle the PO.

The PO was An Príomh Oide, the Principal Teacher, the Principal Officer, or just Pain Number One – according to the different versions I heard during that first week. The students called her Ano. She was the woman responsible for running the big primary and secondary schools, a shrewd, able, odd, busy and thoroughly-complicated woman. If you worked on the staff of Goldenbridge or went to school there – other than in the orphanage which had its own national school – the PO played an insistent and non-negotiable part in your life. The more you got to know her, though she didn't really want you to get to know her, the more complicated she could seem. The chief aim of any junior teacher on the school staff, lay or religious, was to keep out of her range of contemplation. She had a brooding cast of mind. And she loved to play her cards close to her chest so as to make you believe that she had at least a poker of aces to your three deuces.

I think she was a good woman and kind-hearted. She

befriended many people, especially many struggling women and their families, in moments of real need. And it was she who took the initiative in setting up a free secondary school in Goldenbridge. She did this nearly two decades before second-level education was made available by the state for all Irish children.

But she gave practically everyone in the school – staff, students and parents – a little bit of hell at some time or other. We didn't mind too much getting hell when everybody else was getting it. But, like taking cascara when you were a youngster, we didn't relish swallowing it on the basis that somebody else had decided it was good for us.

Like many women in religious communities in those days who, in obedience to the prevailing orthodoxy, felt they had to supress their sexuality – and not just their sexuality but everything that reminded them that sex still existed – she seemed to have converted her vital urges into the exercise of a kind of prudishly-vigilant power.

A basic kindness in her nature warred sometimes with her perceived mission or comission from Carysfort to turn every black novice into a good, conforming, hard-working subaltern. So she could come at you in different ways. And being a tall, hefty, awkwardly-built woman with darting eyes, she could certainly intimidate you.

Coming to terms with the PO – learning eventually to mark out a small space for respect and self-respect *vis-à-vis* this odd, forceful and uneasy woman whose sense of life was so different from mine – took me nearly the whole of my five years in Goldenbridge. But it was an exercise that would stand me in good stead. I was to meet situations that called for the same effort, again and again.

The PO dropped me off that first Friday morning – the day after I arrived in Goldenbridge – in Kevin's classroom. It was a strategic move. The classroom was next door to her own office. She must have given me a few instructions about how to handle the sixty-five Infants she was confiding to my care that morning. But I wasn't able to turn her advice to any practical account. My fright, after the first few minutes, was too great.

Did you ever feel utterly helpless and inadequate? Did you ever confront a small restless mass of humanity confined in a high-walled, stuffy place? Did you ever feel a desperate, rising panic? Did you ever mind two or three energetic four-year-olds for a day? Did you ever, as a rookie teacher, try to mind sixty-five...?

When I survived that Friday and the few weeks that followed it, I felt that nothing worse could ever happen to me or to the children again. And I could understand why Kevin kept a big stick on her table. It was supposed to be a pointer for the blackboard... I felt safer using the ruler.

By the time Kevin came back there were sixty-nine pupils in the classroom. It was the time of year for taking in new pupils. I had always suspected that I wasn't cut out to be a teacher of small children. Now I was certain. So it was a relief of sorts when the beginning of the new school year came around and I was assigned to teach Standard Five in the classroom with the sinking foundations. It wasn't a bad year, but it wasn't a great one either. I had to face the final inspection for my teacher's diploma. I had growing doubts about my vocation to be a primary teacher. I was nervous and edgy and cross. Pity the poor youngsters who had to put up with me that year.

The good news – it came during the summer holidays, I think – was that the central council of the congregation in Carysfort had decided a group of us should enrol as night students at the university. We were odd fish in the university too, even though religious black – along with a ubiquitous chalky grey and an ingrained, colourless scholarly grime – was a pervasive feature of the decor of Earlsfort Terrace during those years.

We travelled to and from the college in the beginning by taxi – you couldn't have black novices walking the streets of

Dublin at night, Archbishop McQuaid had said. So our Blue Cab was only a shade less conspicuous than the long black chauffeur-driven limousine that dropped and collected the Loreto Sisters from Rathfarnham Abbey during the day.

Goldenbridge was the last stop on our taximan's three-convent run. This meant that we rarely got home before 11.30 p.m. With a bundle of school copies on the table waiting to be corrected, a cookery class to be prepared, and sometimes an essay to start or finish before you turned in – and look sharp again at 5.30 a.m. for community prayers – the life of a junior in Goldenbridge in those days was no bed of petunias.

University College Dublin in the 1950s was nobody's dream of the groves of academe either. But it had its moments, and I think it saved me. From what? Well, from being made over into the likeness of the PO or the Town Planner, for one thing. It also moved me further and further away from the likelihood of ever having to work in an orphanage or even in a primary school, for the rest of my life.

I wouldn't have thought of it that way or put it into those words for myself, back then. Much less would I have confessed it to anybody else even if I had been conscious of it. But looking back now I know that it was an unspoken and comforting truth somewhere in my subconscious during those early and decisive years in Goldenbridge.

THE OLD BARRACKS

It was the PO who brought me on my first visit to one of the flats in Keogh Square. I had walked around the old barracks a few times before that, but I had never been inside any of the flats and I was vaguely afraid because of the reports I had heard about some of them.

From the outside the place looked grim and forbidding. A military garrison-headquarters from the early nineteenth century, it had been converted into flats in the 1920s as part of an effort to ease the acute housing shortage that the Irish Free State inherited along with other burdens of independence, when the British left Dublin in 1922. But these old barracks-quarters had long since deteriorated into a warren of dark, ill-smelling tenements that the city authorities would, sooner or later, have to pull down.

Externally the buildings retained all the features of an old military compound. There were high cut-stone arches, originally built for lancers or cavalry, perhaps. The long rectangular dressed-limestone buildings were linked to one another by cobbled yards and paved parade-grounds. And everywhere there were thick walls, high iron railings, and stairways of dark grey stone that wept profusely in damp weather.

Still, I found it almost impossible to imagine the former life of this big military complex – the gleaming instruments of a military band, say, or the elegance of red-jacketed cavalry on parade, or even the spit-and-polish of the khaki-clad infantry who must have lined up here to march to Sunday services in some of the nearby churches. By 1959 the whole appearance of the place had deteriorated into unredeemable squalor and ugliness.

So I walked with a certain timidity behind the PO when she took me with her into the barracks to inquire about two small children who had been missing from school for more than a week. For a big awkward woman the PO was fastidious in some ways. She lifted her long skirts carefully and made a sign for me to do the same. She wrinkled her nose at the heavy odour of stale cooking and excrement that rose to meet us from the shaft of the stairwell when we started climbing. A small boy from First Class, called Christopher, and his sister Mary, aged seven and eight respectively, had been out of school for their eighth successive day. Something would have to be done about it, the PO explained briefly. But there was nobody in the flat when we got to the third floor.

'Mary is gone to her Ma's with the kids,' a neighbour from the other side of the landing told us. 'Kitser is on the tatther again. He bet herself and the young ones up somethin' terrible. That'd be a week last Friday. And young Kit should be makin' his First Communion this year too...'

The door of the empty flat was ajar. It hung sideways off forced hinges and didn't have a lock or a doorknob. It was a one-roomed flat, a big, dark, high-ceilinged room that served as kitchen, living-room and bedroom, all in one. For water and toilet necessities you had to go down two flights of stairs to the landing on the first floor.

There was no sign of a table or a chair in the room, and there was hardly any glass in the lower window-panes. Rags and bits of cardboard kept out the cold and light. A torn, decayed-looking, hair mattress in the far corner near the fireplace had a bundle of rags on top of it, and something that might have been a smaller bundle of rags or a cot-mattress was lying near the damp wall alongside it. In the fireplace there was a heap of cold ashes. A blackened aluminium teapot was the only sign of recent occupation.

The PO made absolutely no comment as we walked down the stairs again and out under the arch facing the road. We crossed the street and went back back to the convent in silence. It was a community fast-day, the eve of Mercy Day, and was intended to be a day of prayer and recollection. The PO was giving me what she thought of as good example.

Regina Assumpta met us on the way in near the side door. She was one of the young professed sisters in the community. She and I were namesakes, in a way, because I was known as Regina Mundi in the community back then.

A forthright Dublin woman from the South Circular Road, this other Regina hadn't much time for the PO's theatricals and sessions of good example. From the porch beside the poor men's door she beckoned me to follow her.

'Come on,' she said, 'your name is on the slate to help me arrange the flowers on the altar for Mercy Day. Let's go into the sacristy.'

'Do many people live like that?' I asked her when the door of the sacristy closed behind us. 'Like those little ones Christopher and Mary over in the barracks, I mean?'

'Too many,' she said. Oh, God help us, far too many...' And she was about to launch into an indignant explanation when she checked herself.

'But try not to think about the barracks today,' she advised me. 'Tomorrow is Mercy Day. Enjoy the bit of freedom you have this weekend. There'll be all the time in the world for Keogh Square and the misery you'll find there, afterwards. It'll be your daily bread from now on. And you'll be lucky if it doesn't break your heart...'
She opened one of the big sacristy presses. 'Here, help me to get down those two big vases from the top shelf.'

They were special heavy brassware that was used only on big feastdays, she explained. They got tarnished with disuse and dampness in between times, so they'd have to be polished. She produced a soft rag and a tin of Brasso and left me at work.

When she opened the door of the outer sacristy and went into the porch where the flowers were left to keep them fresh,

I heard her exclaiming in loud annoyance, 'Well, hell's bells...'
She came back in with the bucket of freshly-cut flowers in
her hand.

'Look,' she said, 'just look what they sent me, and I
distinctly asked for salmon-coloured chrysanthemums and
some big white ones. But just look at the tatty rubbish they
send me – those awful wishy-washy pinks, and those yucky
puces and purples...' She wrinkled her nose in disgust.

'Well, I'm not going to be responsible for putting the likes
of them on the altar for Mercy Day.' She tossed back her veil
with a gesture of strong annoyance.

'I'm going after Athens about it this very minute.' Her
brown eyes flashed. 'She has those lovely salmon-coloured
ones that I picked out yesterday hidden away somewhere in
that precious glass-house of hers. Now I wonder who she's
keeping them for?'

Regina suffered from asthma and had a congenital heart
weakness. She was supposed to avoid exertion. But she was
formidable when she was annoyed. She rolled up her sleeves
now and grasped the bucket of flowers.

'Come on,' she said. 'We're going to get some decent
crysanths for that altar or my name is not Murphy.' And her
whole stocky frame stiffened with determination.

I was still sick at heart after my visit to the barracks, so I
followed her without much enthusiasm. I was timid about
confrontations at the best of times, and I didn't fancy getting
on the wrong side of Athens either, unless it couldn't be
avoided.

'She's good-hearted, but fairly sharp around the edges,'
was the community line on Athanasius, and I already knew it
was accurate. Besides, the pink and purple crysanths in the
bucket looked fine to me. So I followed Regina reluctantly,
trailing as far behind her as I could. When she got to the door
of the greenhouse I hung back. Let them settle this thing
between them without dragging me into it. I have nothing to
do with it, really...

Athens came out of the big glasshouse with a potted azalea in one hand and a small gardening fork in the other. Her long check apron dipped down to one side like a flag at half-mast. When she saw Regina with the bucket of flowers in her hand she raised her head and sniffed the air. Then she closed her lips tightly and cocked an ear skywards as if she were expecting an air raid. She looked from Regina to the chrysanths and back but said nothing.

I retreated behind a corner of the hedge and made myself as scarce as possible to watch the encounter from a safe distance. The indignant opening volley came from Regina and brought an immediate short, sharp blast back from Athens. Then there was a more extended and calculated exchange of fire, then a negotiation, then some bargaining, and finally a settlement.

They went into the big greenhouse together, and Regina emerged not long afterwards with a dozen beautiful snow-white chrysanths and ten of the deep peach-coloured ones she called salmon. They were all soft, luxurious blossoms. Even I had to admit that they looked magnificent compared with the pale pinks and rusty purples that had been in the bucket originally.

And they seemed to glow with a kind of secret triumph on the high altar the next morning, as if some of Regina's vehemence and determination were radiating from them above the gleaming brass vases. They were especially beautiful for a few minutes during the solemn Benediction ceremony when, amid a cloud of incense, a shaft of strong sunlight filtered in through the tall gable window and caught them in a ray of mid-morning brightness.

That was my first Mercy Day in Goldenbridge. Soon afterwards my namesake, Regina, was assigned to the community's new mission in East Africa. She was to spend the rest of her life working among the Kamba people in the drought-ridden Machakos region of Kenya, training teachers to work in the little clay-and-wattle bush schools of the interior.

Gradually I got more used to my new surroundings and began making regular visits to the flats in Keogh Square. Young Christopher and his sister Mary were back in school again and the little boy made his First Communion on schedule. By degrees we learned to find ways around some of the most immediate problems that came up for the children living in the flats.

But I don't think any of us ever got used to the terrible conditions in which some families had to live in Keogh Square in those years. And although most of us had moved on elsewhere by the time it happened, it was a real relief to hear that Dublin Corporation had finally pulled down the old barracks and replaced it with a scheme of purpose-built family flats in the 1970s.

When I think of that other Regina now I sometimes wonder if there are any crysanthemums – salmon-coloured or otherwise – around the cemetery where she's buried in Nairobi. I know there must be frangipani there and bougainvillaea and hibiscus blossoms and the vivid glow of the Kenyan flame tree. And after so many years in Africa, I reckon Regina wouldn't object anymore to the strong reds and pinks and purples of the country where she spent thirty hard-working and dedicated years.

I remembered her one day during my holidays in Dublin in 1992. I was staying in Block 4 of the flats that occupy the site of the old Keogh Square barracks in Inchicore now, and as I was walking through Saint Michael's Estate I noticed a tiny bed of pink flowers in bloom near the site of the flat where the PO had brought me on my first visit to the barracks in 1959.

These weren't salmon-cloloured, and they weren't crysanthemums, but I think even Regina would have agreed that, growing in that particular spot, they represented a small triumph of hope over poverty, of beauty over ugliness. I heard afterwards that they had been planted by a young man from the flats who had taken up gardening while he was serving a prison-sentence. Regina would have understood the sad appropriateness of that, I guess, and so, I feel sure, would anyone else who ever worked in the Mercy community in Goldenbridge.

NEITHER MALE NOR FEMALE

There were five old sisters in the community when I first arrived in Goldenbridge, and in retrospect they seem to sum up something that was very characteristic of the ethos of the place as I knew it in those years before convent life was changed by the reforms of the Second Vatican Council. They are the ones I think of first when I look back on Goldenbridge as a quintessential product of post-Catholic Emancipation Ireland.

They were in their late seventies or early eighties when I knew them but most of them were still active in some small job or other. They were an odd, in some ways quite an eccentric bunch of individuals. And although they were homogeneously encased within the same black habit, and lived inside the walls of the same convent – where they knew now they'd end their days – they were as different from each other, and as full of an odd, quirky, individual life, as could well be imagined.

Easily the most memorable of them for me, possibly because she came from a family of titled gentry in County Offaly, was Fidelis. Or, as the PO, who was also from that part of the country, used to call her, 'one of the Miss Yarrs'. Goldenbridge was the first place I had ever lived under the same roof with someone from that class of society, and I was prepared to feel a certain awe. The experience was different, and often very funny.

Fidelis was one of those women known in the jargon of the Mercy communities of an earlier day as 'a lady from her own home'. This was a euphemism for someone who had brought the convent a dowry but wasn't qualified for any particular work such as teaching or nursing, cooking or cleaning. This didn't mean that she wouldn't work in a school or hospital or kitchen – although the latter would have been an unusual assignment for such a lady, except in some supervisory capacity.

I don't know what work Fidelis did during her earlier life, but when I knew her she had the job of 'minding the poor men'. These were semi-vagrant gentlemen of all ages, qualities and conditions. They were out of work, out of jail, out of the pub, out of the big psychiatric asylum in Grangegorman, and certainly out of luck, every last one of them. They came to the convent door, day after day, looking for a meal and 'a bit of help'.

Fidelis had taken a liking to them and used to entertain them with mugs of hot tea and slices of buttered bread and whatever else she could get, licitly or illicitly, from the kitchen or the community dining-room. The poor men's base was a little room at the side door near the entrance to the chapel. The superior euphemistically called it the 'poor men's parlour'.

I suppose some poor women came there too but they belonged more properly to Mother Patrick's domain, the social-service kitchen and family food-centre that operated from an old building at the far end of the secondary school near the back gate.

Mother Patrick was a retired superior, an astute and charitable old Corkwoman. She had far more clout and experience when it came to securing resources for her poor women than Fidelis had for her poor men. So, above a certain base line, the latter had to shift in whatever ways she could, to come by some little extras for her clients. They had names like Thomas Ronald Lockhart, The Skin, Baldy, Jomo, Beardy, Edser and Skate.

When she was running short, or if she spotted a favourable opportunity when the superior wasn't around, Fidelis would nip into the refectory and take whatever food she found handy. Or, sensing a shortage coming, she'd find a way to fill the deep pockets of her check apron to capacity with goods out of the community stores. This used to drive the Town Planner wild. These were separate accounting departments...

Fidelis would retort, muttering something under her breath about the dogs being better-fed in this house than the poor men – a reference to the Town Planner's watchdog, a well-groomed, testy German shepherd called Tosca to whom she fed regular titbits and, now and then, a sweet.

Those sweets were a source of grievance among the junior members of the community too; we could have done with a few of them. Our ration was a maximum of six sweets per week, and none at all in Lent or Advent. I don't know if Tosca was made to keep the seasons of ecclesiastical austerity the same as the rest of us. Given the literalness of the Town Planner's way of thinking on many issues, it's quite possible. There was an unspoken philosophy in Convents of Mercy in those days that what you took for yourself by way of a small treat, you were denying to some poor or needy person. Fidelis's view was that what you took from the convent refectory you were taking from the Town Planner's dog. This added spice to her forays, and fuelled the war between herself and the superior.

One Saturday night I was on my way to bed, with a hot-water bottle under one arm and some freshly-ironed laundry on the other. As I turned the corner near the landing I heard Kevin knocking loudly on Fidelis's door.

'Have you my *Mail* in there?' she shouted in her most accusing voice. Apart from *The Irish Times*, Kevin's other favourite reading was *The Dublin Evening Mail*, and it used to drive her into a small fury when Fidelis or one of the others took it in at the hall door and made off to bed with it.

'I have neither male nor female in here,' I heard Fidelis shouting back, 'and you'd be better off without that oul' *Mail* of yours at this hour of the night too. Now go to bed, will you, and leave me in peace.'

I know that, in retrospect, I see those old ladies in a kindlier light than people who lived and worked with them in some earlier and possibly sharper phase of their existence. Even their eccentricities gain in mellowness by not having to be lived with any more.

They remind me, in a way, of my old Bunowen neighbour, Pat. I was greatly afraid of him when I was a child, and so were most of my friends. He had a sharp tongue and a menacing stick. He also had an implacable animus against anyone who had ever tried to rob his orchard – which was practically everyone in the village.

And then, one day, at the end of October – it was the year before he died, I think, and I was eight or nine at the time – he stopped me unexpectedly on the road outside his house on my way home from the sea.

'You can go in there and take all the apples you like,' he said, pointing to the open door of his apple store. First I thought it was a trick. I stood off at a safe distance, wary of taking him at his word. But something in the way he looked, an old man standing there inviting me to take his prized apples, convinced me in the end.

I had no bag so I stripped off my cardigan, tied the ends and sleeves together and filled it to sagging-point with all the apples I could carry. The old man pointed out different ones I could take, small sweet red ones, hard juicy greens, and the big golden dessert apples that turned out to be better to look at than to eat.

No one would believe me when I arrived home and told them where I got the apples. And when I told my brother Johnny, back from the USA, about it many years later, he said 'I wouldn't believe you either. That oul' fellow was the most cantankerous bastard any good man ever had for a neighbour. And I should know.'

I couldn't argue with that, although the word 'provocation' flickered across my mind. My brother Johnny, as a young man, wasn't exactly an eager farmer or a model keeper of drains and boundary fences. But Pat had a sharp and complaining tongue and often threw a bitter word after you as you passed down the road. There was no denying that.

And yet when I think of him now, what I remember is not my fear of his raised stick, nor the sharp scoldings he gave me and my friends over the years, but that miraculous haul of Hallowe'en apples. I suppose I think of the old nuns in Goldenbridge in something the same way.

SHADOWS

The day I came up from school and saw my name on the slate to take my turn at minding Mother Patrick, my heart sank. Not that I didn't want to mind the poor sick woman, but I was nervous. She was probably dying, and in everything to do with death or serious illness, I was inexperienced.

Growing up as the youngest of a family of nine had its advantages, but also its drawbacks. Usually the small chores like washing dishes, running for messages, bringing in turf for the fire, rounding up the cows for milking, and the like, were passed on to me by my older brothers and sisters. But when it came to more responsible jobs like entertaining visitors or coping with sickness in the family, the opposite was true.

There was relatively little serious illness in my family during the years when I was growing up, and there had been no death in the immediate household since I was born. When my mother had to have surgery and was diagnosed as a diabetic needing daily injections, or when my father discharged himself from hospital, impatient with his treatment there, they were looked after by my older sisters.

So here I was at the age of twenty-three, diffident and inexperienced, taking my turn at minding a very elderly woman who was dying of cancer. At the beginning she wasn't completely helpless so I grew into the job by degrees. It was only a matter of a few hours in the morning or evening anyway.

I was curious about death now, and I was curious about old Patrick too. She had been a figure of some importance in the community, a capable and charitable woman who was superior of several convents including some of the biggest in the city. She had built extensions to the Mater Hospital and Saint Michael's in Dun Laoghaire in the days when grants were not available from the Department of Health, and money had to be raised by the ingenuity of the person in charge of the project.

She was also a woman about whom stories of small miracles of charity in her dealings with needy people were regularly told. How a poor man came looking for a pair of boots on a snowy night and she gave him the last pound note in the drawer - and then a cheque from an anonymous donor came by post the following morning. How she gave the community Christmas cake to a poor family on Christmas Eve – and the community wasn't prepared to thank her for it – but then a Christmas cake was delivered at the door as a gift from Kennedy's Bakery late that same evening. Stories like that.

She was an astute and resourceful woman, and I knew that some members of the community claimed that she had enjoyed being a figure of authority in her day even if a capable, conscientious and responsible one. I don't know when exactly it had come about that a sort of *de facto* sphere of separateness was established with regard to the running of the industrial school in Goldenbridge. By the end of Mother Patrick's life, the convent community played practically no direct role in the day-to-day workings of the school, except to supply the sisters who worked there. In a more perfect world this wouldn't have been a bad thing. In Carysfort many years later I was glad that there was no interference from the convent in the running of the training college. It would have been inappropriate.

What Goldenbridge and other Irish industrial schools lacked in the 1950s, apart from any kind of near-adequate financing, were such structures as boards of management and independent forms of external supervision and assessment which might have acted as supports and guarantees for the day-to-day quality of service. It would be at the insistence of the schools themselves – and Goldenbridge was one of the leaders in this regard – that the state would eventually agree to broaden the system of management and put in better forms of training, staffing and professional support for the child-care service.

After her retirement as superior Mother Patrick had concentrated her efforts on the food centre where free meals were served to expectant mothers and needy families. I often saw her on a cold day pulling her shawl around her and heading out into the rain and wind to go down to the centre which was located near the back gate. It wasn't a comfortable place to work, an old building hard to heat, with sticky floors and steamed-up windows on damp days. Some people referred to it disparagingly as the Soup Kitchen. But Mother Patrick remained faithful to her work and her friends there until she could no longer manage to walk down to it. At that point she took to her bed.

And now she was dying, and I used to sit beside her bed, anxious to help her but unable to do anything to ease that laboured breathing. And I'd wonder how it felt at the end for someone who had exercised authority in her day and had done all the good she could, but had to hand in her ticket at the last turnstile now like everyone else.

She had been a woman of prayer and had followed the guidance of spiritual directors in her time. She had read the spiritual classics and was known in old age for her fluent command of ascetical terminology.

'Man's destiny is wonderful,' she said to me one night as I was sitting by the bed. She repeated the phrase a few times and then tried to elaborate on it. But her words didn´t register any immediate meaning for me. It was as if she were trying to convince someone – whether herself or me I wasn't sure. And I think I sensed then that the real achievement of this woman had relatively little to do with words, especially the abstract phrases of piety that came to her from books and devotional reading. Her achievement lay rather in what she had done in impoverished times to improve hospitals and nursing care for people who were too poor to pay for them, and in her help for sick and suffering people of all kinds, and above all in the practical kindnesses she had shown to homeless and hungry families in their times of need. The words she was using now were like something that came from outside her, and even back then – when I still had a novice's cautious regard for words of piety – that seemed to me to be, somehow, a pity.

It was very near the end, in fact a week or so before she died, that the episode of the teeth took place. She had asked us to make sure her false teeth were put in before the priest came up to give her Holy Communion in the morning, and taken out again immediately afterwards. They were heavy and uncomfortable now for her shrunken gums.

We told this incident so often afterwards I can't be sure whether it was Marie or Patsy or Carmel and myself – the black novices on the rota at the time – who did the taking out, or attempted taking out, of the teeth. The top plate slipped away easily enough, but the bottom one was stubborn. We tugged and shifted, lifted and angled the jaw a bit and pulled sideways, but nothing happened. The bottom teeth, of course, were her own. They weren't going to come out with any amount of tugging.

The thing reflected no credit on us. But it was a sort of lesson to me. A once-powerful woman at the mercy of a couple of clumsy, well-meaning youngsters – and she couldn't even bite back...

Mother Patrick died that spring. The iced cake with green lettering saying 'Happy Feastday' that Ita and Catherine had made for her before Saint Patrick's Day sat on a shelf in the pantry for a week or more. Nobody seemed keen to to eat it – a miracle in those hungry times – but nobody wanted to throw it out either. It probably went, in the end, to Fidelis's poor men.

If she had been buried in the DOM with a lapidary phrase

on her tombstone like the Queen's Counsellor or the Member of the Paving Board, the legend might have read, 'A Sister of Mercy cast in the Classic Mould'. As it was, she got the little iron cross that was customary for a sister in those days, with her name and date of religious profession painted in black on it. And long years afterwards, these random memories swirling like morning mist on a hill in distant Valparaiso...

The day old Avellino fell on her rear end among the Town Planner's prize tulips was a rough day for everyone. This impressive bed of tulips had been planted with special bulbs that the TP had sent away for. They had grown into fine tall blossoms, standing upright like colourful chalices on sturdy stems. A great deal of care and patience had gone into cultivating them. So the TP was in wicked humour, not least because she suspected – correctly – that the catastrophe wasn't being viewed with the same seriousness by everyone in the community.

Like Fidelis, Avellino was an old lady with a personality very much her own. She was another of the five very elderly women who lived in the Goldenbridge community when I first arrived there. She may well have been a hard-working and industrious individual when she was younger – though I couldn't quite imagine it. In her old age, at any rate, she had developed the ways of a lady of leisure, and an independent-minded, peripatetic and slightly provocative one at that.

The Town Planner, I think, reckoned that Avie had been sent by providence as a special trial to her patience, and a challenge to her authority – or at least to her ingenuity. Avie was quite old and frail at this time, a soft-spoken, gently-smiling woman with a mischievous glint in her eye. She had a graceful but, by now, very stooped figure, and she walked with the help of a stick. And walk she did, everywhere, even when she was reduced to getting about with the help of a metal tripod.

The TP had cleared a small parlour and made a comfortable bedroom for her downstairs near the dining-room. But Avie insisted on climbing the stairs, regularly, to the upper floor. Maybe she wanted to see the view. At any rate she fell down the stairs a couple of times. We used to think she had rubber bones because, in spite of numerous bruises, she survived every fall.

Avellino had an old friend called Juliana, a member of the Mater hospital community. In their younger days they had the reputation – in spite of strict convent horaria and the constant vigilance of superiors – of getting around a bit. They were still inclined to attempt the odd expedition even in old age, and once in a while it landed them in trouble.

Like the day they found themselves several miles from base, with the deadline for the locking of the convent gates only twenty minutes away. They had no money for a taxi. So they feigned distress, flagged down a passing police car – and made it to the convent dead on the stroke of curfew. All would have been well and no one any the wiser, only that the young man who was driving the squad car happened to have a sister in the community...

If the TP had cause against Avie before that, she felt she had hanging evidence against her now. So on the day of the tulips she wasn't inclined to pull her punches. She fairly laid into the old lady. The bed of tulips was just outside one of the big windows of the community room, and there happened to be a witness...

When she had picked Avie up out of the flowers, dusted her down, and put her back on her walking-aid, she let her have the length and breadth of her tongue. She went on and on, and made several detours into history including the episode of the squad car.

Avie listened patiently, even sweetly, an expression of gentle inquiry playing across her features. In the meantime she was slowly drawing her stooped figure up to its full height until she stood with a slim, upright dignity nobody had seen in her for years. A tall woman in her day, she looked down now at the short, purple-faced TP.

When the latter had finished sounding off, Avie turned slowly as if to walk away in dignified silence. But then, gazing back over her shoulder at the irate little superior, she inquired in her softest tones, 'Have you any further charges to bring against me? I was merely picking a few flowers.'

The last of the five very old ladies living in Goldenbridge when I came there was a woman from Newry called Elizabeth MacAllister. She had charge of the poultry, and spent a good part of her time down at the sheds we called the hen-run.

I replaced her on the job once when she went away for a retreat or a holiday. After that, although she wasn't a very talkative woman, we had an understanding and a topic of conversation, so we became good friends.

The PO who liked to make arch jokes, asked me one day if I wasn't planning to become a Bachelor of Eggs as well as a Bachelor of Arts. I said, no, though I might be interested in a Master's degree in the subject. I had served my time to the basic grades long ago, following the hem of my mother's skirt around the yard and henhouse in Bunowen.

LOSS AND LEARNING

In May 1960 when I was almost a year in Goldenbridge and still teaching Standard Five in the national school, my father died. It was a lonely and very painful time for me.

I had been close to him as a child, a small girl trailing behind him through fields and meadows and around the barn and stable and cowhouse. He was fifty-eight when I was born, a grandfather-figure when I knew him who had more patience with me, the youngest, than he had with any of my older siblings, or so I was told.

But during my teenage years at boarding school I had grown away from him. At thirteen I was vaguely uncomfortable among my classmates about having a father who was a stooped old countryman in his seventies wearing a hat and working clothes so battered they looked as if Noah had discarded them from the ark. I wasn't able to make much conversation with him when I came home from school on holidays either.

So, in 1956 when I finished teacher-training in Carysfort and announced that I wanted to enter the novitiate there, he couldn't understand it. He was seventy-seven at the time, and what he had heard about nuns when he was young was that they went into the convent because they 'couldn't get a man'. There was a sister in the local convent with whom he did business occasionally about poached salmon – my father, even in his older years, was a nifty poacher. It was said of her that 'she joined the nuns on Black Pat'. For spite on him, we supposed.

So the convent, to my father's way of thinking, was mostly 'a refuge for jilted judies'. And he couldn't understand how his youngest daughter, not yet twenty, could think of burying herself in a place like that. He put all the pressure he could on me, but I had my mother's support. She was an admirer and friend of the Louisburgh Sisters of Mercy who had taught us in school. She had even named me Teresita after one of them. And the light shining in the convent chapel every morning before six o'clock – visible like a small beacon from our kitchen window as she got up to light the fire – had always been a source of comfort and reassurance for her. So I got my way, and left Bunowen for Carysfort in September 1956.

Four years later, when the news of my father's death reached me in Goldenbridge, what I remembered, along with his strong opposition to my entering the convent, was his grief the morning I set out for the novitiate, and the stubble on his chin as he kissed me goodbye, and the familiar scent of pipe-tobacco from his clothes – and the sad, uncomprehending look in his eyes.

I never saw him again. We weren't allowed to go home on visits to our family in those years, and he was too old and bent to travel to Dublin. Novices weren't given leave to attend family funerals either. So I sat in my room, after the community had expressed its sympathy, alone with my grief and my regrets.

I was passing the pantry the day after his death when I overheard Sister Teresa Agnes telling the PO that she had heard me sobbing out loud in my bedroom. I wasn't aware that I had been crying aloud. I felt she was shocked at my lack of restraint. I didn't care.

It took me months to recover from whatever it was that my father's death unleashed in me. It took me years to begin to understand him a little, in retrospect. And it has taken me decades to reach the stage where I'm grateful to have inherited some small part of his silence, his sanity, and his saving scepticism.

I never came to share his views about the convent being a refuge for jilted judies, though. Our situation seemed to me to be a good deal more interesting than that, and our motivations were certainly more unconscious and complex. It would be many years before I'd understand why I had, quite appropriately for someone of my temperament and orientation, entered a religious community at the age of nineteen. By then I was about ready to leave it.

Sure we were screwed up when it came to recognising – much less expressing – our ordinary biological and vital urges. In the 1950s we didn't even talk about the chastity we had taken a vow to 'practise', never mind the sex it put out of bounds even in our heads. But youth is resourceful – unconsciously when it can't be otherwise. And there are few people quite so good at high-voltage sublimation as a youngster such as I was back then, reading spiritual classics on the one hand, and English literature on the other – and, ah yes, sitting in admiration at the feet of the recently-returned, erotically-enhanced Denis D. who was lecturing us on Keats' Odes in UCD in the evenings.

Enhanced? By our awe of his rapier-sharp intellect, his sojourn among the New Critics in the USA, the loftiness of his disdain, the dexterity of his language, and the exciting clarity of his critical insights. What matter that the Physics Theatre in Earlsfort Terrace was crammed to the rafters with hundreds of indifferently motivated night students. The debonair young English lecturer would have cut a commanding figure in any setting.

There weren't too many of his calibre in UCD at the time. But when Robin Dudley Edwards from the History Department made one of his rare, vatic appearances among his night students, you could also feel the subliminal vibrations of what you fondly supposed was the intellectual life.

Afterwards when a fine, probing, ironic text like Chaucer's *Troilus and Criseyde* turned up on the course, you had a real tool in your hands, at least for analytic and speculative purposes. Its five books took you through the old Trojan love saga - sight, pursuit, intrigue and seduction, to tender nights of dalliance in Criseyde's bed and the lovers' lingering aubades. And from there, all the way around again to separation, betrayal, disabusement, and the painful exaltation of Troilus's final, bitter-sweet rejection of carnal love – which in, Chaucer's telling of the tale, is, of course, posthumous.

The last pages of the poem – a dozen or so verses out of five substantial books, it's true, but what matter, I was prepared to be persuaded – seemed to be a confirmation of everything a good novice ever believed... or wanted to believe:

> Oh all you fresh young people, he or she,
> In whom love grows and ripens year by year,
> Come home, come home from worldly vanity!
> Cast the heart's countenance in love and fear
> Upwards to God, who in His image here
> Has made you; think this world is but a fair
> Passing as soon as flower-scent in the air.
>
> And give your love to Him who, for pure love,
> Upon a cross first died that He might pay
> Our debt, and rose, and sits in Heaven above;
> He will be false to no one that will lay
> His heart wholly on Him, I dare to say.
> Since he is best to love, and the most meek,
> What need is there for feigning love to seek?

Ah, the anguished, comforting, melancholy self-contradictions of youth! Like Troilus – or Saint Augustine, or Chaucer, or whoever – it was consoling to be able to go through the kind of ascetical and aesthetical manouevrings that showed you what you might be missing, and then intimated how beautifully worthless the hero considered it all – after he died. And so, in a speculative sense at least, you ended up by with a small savour of it both ways.

Cecilia Xavier who taught in the national school with me

that first year, was a tall Galway woman with a big heart. She was a friend and buddy of Kevin, and she worried about me because she found me sceptical on the subject of love.

Well, walking around in a long black habit and coping with a seventeen-or eighteen-hour working day, what was the point of me getting worked up about love just then? And scepticism was as good a cover as any.

But Cecilia took love seriously – divine love, human love, family love. She often tried to straighten me out on the subject, over the dishes in the washtub after meals. Dolorita, another Galway woman, and Regina of the salmon-coloured chrysanthemums would play umpire and referee for us.

'It's mostly a lot of hoo-haa,' I'd say, 'and not half what it's cracked up to be. If you ask me, it's just a question of enlightened self-interest....'

I had learned that useful phrase in a history lecture in UCD. The Enlightened Despots in eighteenth-century Europe were good at it - the self-interest and the styles of love that went with it.

'Oh, no,' Cecilia would say earnestly, 'you mustn't talk like that. Love is what life is all about. God himself is Love. It's love that moves the sun and all the stars. Saint John of the Cross says that at the end of life we'll all be judged on love.... Regina, dear, you must learn to love.'

I had every intention of it – when I had time. But I hadn't time yet. Love, like leisure, would have to wait a bit. My life was far too full and busy at the moment; which gave rise to a theory I held for some time afterwards – that you could get several good years of dedication, hard work, and fairly genuine celibacy out of a willing and well-motivated young person – three or five years, or maybe even seven or ten, depending on the individual and the climate – if you kept them suitably occupied and agreeably challenged, their juices flowing, so to speak, in other engaging directions.

But after that you were likely to run into problems. And even those like myself whose useful little carapace of scepticism was often a cover for devout and serious strivings – I was inclined to want it both ways – had to face the growing sense of discord, the felt dissonance between the inner music of experience and what came, on verbal authority, from outside, on the subject of celibacy.

After that you either had to decide to block off your vital system at certain points, control things, keep some areas out of bounds – and so consent to let a part of you die or gradually atrophy. Or else you kept all systems functional but on a sort of stop-go basis for which you suffered agonies of useless remorse afterwards. Oh, we were screwed up all right.

I already knew it could go that way, knew it in my guts if not in my head, and I was glad, while I was in Goldenbridge, to put off the hour of reckoning. But I enjoyed playing little games of verbal ping-pong with Cecilia about love, over the washtub, while a knowing Dolorita and an amused Regina played chorus for us in the background. It was another of the vicarious little ways we had of writing off our immediate losses.

What matter that a small group of us were still trailing in and out of Earlsfort Terrace – not in a taxi anymore but on the No. 20 bus to Harcourt Street – wearing long black habits, and eating our biscuits in the dank bowels of UCD. The sandwiches that Ita prepared for me in Goldenbridge I ate amid the dripping pipes and boiler-house gloom of the basement, in what was called the Nuns' Room. It was a place of sombre light and melancholy decor. But the labour we delight in physicks pain, and I, for one, wasn't averse to the discomforts my studies brought me. They seemed to me to be part of a reasonable package.

Back in Goldenbridge it was still a question of trying to steer clear of the vigilance of the PO, or of escaping from the endless chores devised by the Town Planner who believed – on the authority of a phrase from the Mercy Rule – that 'idleness teaches much evil'. Studying 'secular subjects' was still considered a near relation to idleness. So, finding a shady tree in a quiet part of the orchard, or escaping to the old laundry 'bleach' near the back gate to get an hour's peace to read, or to plan an essay, or just to have a quiet conversation with a friend, was still something of an escapade.

I remember promising myself that when the pressures of study were over I'd sit down and actually read those history books that I was having to skim through now to collect material for essays. It was a worthy intention. But it would soon be overtaken by more pressing events.

ONE HOUR AHEAD OF THE POSSE

In 1960 the superior general in Carysfort accepted an invitation from an Irish-American bishop to send teaching sisters from the Dublin Mercy communities to staff a Catholic parish school in Gadsden in the diocese of Mobile in Alabama. Sister Mary, who had been teaching history to the Leaving Cert class in Goldenbridge, was one of those assigned to go, and I was drafted at short notice to replace her as a history teacher in the secondary school.

It was the first time – apart from my brief sojourn among Kevin's Infants – that I found myself in what looked like a serious cabbages-upside-down situation. Not that I didn't like history. Not that I hadn't chosen it as one of my degree subjects in the university. It was just that I had never studied – and so was entirely ignorant of – the specific courses assigned by the Department of Education in alternating years for Leaving Cert students in the early 1960s.

One was a course in medieval history, full of Ottos, Henrys and Fredericks, Holy Roman Emperors quarrelling with imperially-minded Popes with names like Gregory, Innocent and Boniface, about abstruse matters such as lay investiture and spheres of spiritual and temporal authority – which I gradually understood was about power, wealth, land, influence...

And the other was a seventeenth-century course, replete with religious wars, Irish rebellions and land settlements, the grasping follies of the Stuarts, and the exorbitant vanities of their cousin, the 'Sun King' of France. Not a word about B Specials anywhere – unless they could have been prognosticated by some uncannily prescient crystal ball-gazer, as one of the many troublesome outcomes of King

William's victory at the Battle of the Boyne in the War of the League of Augsburg....

Being called on to teach a Leaving Certificate honours history course, without the minimum preparation, was a difficult situation in which to find myself a few weeks before the start of the school year. So I took my case to the novice-mistress. She had said, after all, 'Peace, but not peace at all costs.'

The costs, I argued, would be too high for the current crop of Leaving Cert students, and they'd certainly be too high for me, coming on top of a day's work in school and evening classes at the university. In a year's time, I promised, I'd make shape to do a reasonable job on the following year's courses, having had some time to prepare them.

She listened sympathetically, and then said she was sorry but there wasn't a thing she could do about it. If I liked she'd have a word with the PO, and if I liked I could do the same. But she didn't hold out much hope of a favourable response. The PO had her problems too, she said.

I don't know what the novice-mistress said to the PO. And I don't remember exactly what I said to her either. But I do remember very clearly the frustration I felt coming out of her office that day. I walked around the cemetery in the evening, around it and around it.... And I walked there again, alone, for several evenings afterwards.

The formula that finally reconciled me to attempting the impossible – because it was unavoidable – on that occasion probably came to me during one of those solitary walks around the cemetery. I had occasion to draw on it many times afterwards. I still call it to mind occasionally. It came from a story in the English Reader we were using in Standard Five when I taught in the school with the sinking foundations.

The story was about an oriental king whose chief counsellor offended his sovereign and got into his very bad graces. The king sentenced him to instant and irrevocable banishment. The counsellor pleaded. His friends at court interceded. The king relented – a little. He said 'I'll give you one year – twelve months from today – during which time you must teach my horse to fly. If you fail, your head comes off at the end of the twelve months. Pht.'

The counsellor reflected and then accepted the king's offer. His friends were aghast. 'How could you do such a stupid thing?' they asked him.

'Well,' said the counsellor, 'This is how I see it. Before the end of the year one of a number of things could happen. The king might die. Or I might die. Or the horse might learn to fly...'

And that's how it came about that I spent the summer of 1960 cramming seventeenth-century history down my throat with unseemly and indigestible haste. That's also how I came to spend a whole school year trying to stay a few steps ahead of a Leaving Cert class who – I knew – knew more about seventeenth-century history when we started the year than I did.

And that's how I learned to keep one hour ahead of the posse – by urging my timorous little horse to fly.

I was to discover afterwards that throwing you in at the deep end was one of the PO's favourite strategies with junior staff, a sort of baptism by immersion. She threw you in the deep water and you came up baptised whether you liked it or not.

It happened much like that the time Sister Columba, the Art teacher in the secondary school, was transferred to Arklow. The PO decided that Teresa Margaret and myself should take over her Inter Cert Art classes. I think the subject was called Drawing back then.

We were a pair of young national teachers recently out from Carysfort. In the training college you got a basic introduction to art, mostly in the form of a utility-course in blackboard drawing. But that didn't seem to bother the PO. Her only problem was that she had to get us 'approved' by an inspector from the Departmant of Education in order to teach in the secondary school.

So she called us into her office one Saturday morning and told us we were to 'assemble a portfolio', one each. We were to present it, and ourselves, to Mr Ó Máille on Monday morning at eleven o' clock.

I had been a fairly willing doodler for as long back as I could remember. I had doodled, in my time, with the shapes of soldiers' caps – that was World War Two or my brother Johnny in the FCA; with horses in movement – I liked riding and watching my father's mare when I was little; landscapes and a lake with swans – that was from my years in boarding school in Tourmakeady on the shores of Lough Mask. Later I added trees, clouds, fence-posts, rabbits, houses, mountains, church spires and jugs to my repertoire. I tended to avoid the human figure. It seldom looked human in any recognised proportions by the time I was finished with it.

I don't know what I presented to Mr Ó Máille in my portfolio that Monday morning. He can't have been impressed, but he 'approved' me anyway. He probably knew that the PO wouldn't have press-ganged the likes of me into teaching Art if she had any decent alternative.

The interesting thing was that the PO's hunches about us sometimes paid off. In time I would become a reasonable teacher of History, and in the Art and Crafts area Teresa Margaret – or Carmel as we were to call her later – turned out to have a real future. She went on to study at the National College of Art and later at the Pratt Institute in New York. I, on the other hand, retired gratefully from teaching Drawing at the end of the year.

The PO dropped me off at the deep end of the pier for an unwanted swim on another occasion too. This was shortly after I first arrived in Goldenbridge in 1959.

There was a Girls' Club attached to the convent in those years, a sort of social get-together with crafts and cookery, book-keeping, music and other classes for youngsters who'd had to leave school early. It met a few nights a week in a hall at the far end of the secondary school near the back gate.

The PO used it as a place for pep-talks and 'instruction' – with the reasonable idea of trying to put off as long as possible the foreclosing moment when a sixteen-year-old became pregnant and the unpropitious cycle started all over again and was fastened down for another generation.

Occasionally she arranged a retreat for the girls in the club, and she happened to have one going on the first Sunday after I arrived in Goldenbridge. She detailed me to take a session with a group of the younger ones while she was busy elsewhere.

Out from the novitiate with fervour all over my face, I had one idea of what a retreat should be. Out for the day to have a couple of free meals and a bit of craic together, the club-girls had a different one. And as we'd say in Mayo they made a hare of me.

An innocent sheep out from Carysfort to be shorn – a lamb with a real woolly fleece! They fell to with a will. I won't say they did it cruelly, but they certainly had a good time shearing me. It passed the day so agreeably for them they used to tell stories about it afterwards.

But I was so put down by the experience it was a long time before I could even talk to anyone about it. And from then on I had my reservations about the value of religious retreats as a means of reclaiming wayward teenagers to virtue.

What I did admire was how the PO and other sisters on the staff, who had worked hard all day in school, went out again at night to take part in the sessions with the girls in the club. They too had to roll out for prayers the next morning when the convent call-bell rang at 5.30 a.m.

PRAYERBOOKS TO COMPUTERS

Stella came back to Goldenbridge on holidays from her mission school in Kenya in the summer of 1962. It was her first time to come on home leave from Africa, and she was collecting prayerbooks to take back with her.

The Mercy mission in Kenya, where many young Goldenbridge sisters were assigned to work during those years, had been started in Nairobi in 1956, and it was the dream of many of us who were young at the time to go out and work there.

I had a vivid memory of the first time I saw two sisters being sent off to Nairobi from Carysfort while I was still a white novice. We lined up on either side of the wide corridor near the hall door and sang 'Go Ye Afar' – a missionary hymn of high aspirations though set in a mournful minor key. We had borrowed it from the Holy Ghost Fathers, I think.

It was a difficult time in Kenya, the decade before independence. The Mau Mau, Jomo Kenyatta's freedom fighters, were at the height of their pre-independence activity. The country, still a part of British East Africa, was in turmoil. Killings and burnings on white settler stations were making headlines in the press. Our little group of missionary sisters, a small band setting out for the dangers that might confront them in such a country, were the nearest thing we knew to living heroines.

I don't know if they were aware before they went of the special kinds of corruption that flourish in the dying days of empires. It would be years before I read a description of the Kenya of that epoch as 'a place in the sun for shady people' – shady white colonial people, it was implied, at that particular point in the country's history.

Stella and her companions were to live through the tensions and conflicts of those turbulent years not just in Kenya's history but in Africa's. It was a moment of high hopes and intense political excitement. New states were coming to birth all across the continent. They were days of euphoria and heady expectation and, inevitably, of disappointment.

The Sisters of Mercy made the small practical contribution they were skilled at initiating in a struggling country, new to its independence and trying to get on its feet. They built a Mater Hospital in Nairobi city, opened schools and clinics in poor urban areas, ran mobile clinics and rural schools and organised a small training college for teachers in the bush. They saw their mission primarily as a spiritual thing. When she came home to Goldenbridge that first time, after all, Stella was still collecting prayerbooks.

But in the early 1960s people in Ireland weren't quite ready yet to part with their prayerbooks, at least not with their good prayerbooks. So what she got was a collection of yellowy, well-thumbed, sweaty, clapped-out little volumes, or old, small-print, brownish ones that had been published in Pater Noster Row in London at the end of the nineteenth century. Most of them looked as if they had been well sneezed on and drowsed over at one time or another but hadn't seen active service for many a year now.

Stacked up in a corner of Stella's bedroom they began to grow into an untidy, almost menacing pile. I watched them increasing in number and variety until they began, for some reason, to remind me of the rats in *The Pied Piper of Hamelin*:

> Great rats, small rats, lean rats, brawny rats,
> Brown rats, black rats, grey rats, tawny rats...

By the time her holidays were over Stella had so many old prayerbooks in that little room, she couldn't think of bringing more than a fraction of them back with her. She wasn't going by sea this time. The days of air travel and baggage restrictions had arrived.

So it fell to the rest of us to get rid of the mouldy surplus when she was gone. We were afraid, I think, that the musty old clutter might bring real rats about the place. We set to shortly after she left to deal with the situation.

First we stuffed the discarded prayerbooks into big canvas sacks. Then we looked for a tar-barrel, the biggest one we could find. A neighbour who was working in the road maintenance section of Dublin Corporation obliged us with a fairly sizeable one. It had small scrapings of tar left in the bottom and along the sides. These, we optimistically thought, would help us to get a better blaze going. Someone bored air-holes in it, and we were ready to start.

We picked a windy corner of the back yard where we figured the cross-draughts might help to fan a good brisk flame, and one autumn evening after school we filled the barrel with the contents of the first sack. We laid them down loosely in separate layers with a row of air-holes and balled-up newspapers between each set of splayed prayerbooks. It was a bit like making a marble-cake, the dark layers and the lighter-coloured ones alternating. The light ones were the big balls of newspaper soaked in paraffin that we were using as kindling.

Finally we lit the bonfire. The newspapers caught fire immediately and went up like some flaring dream of the ephemeral. But we had no previous experience of burning prayerbooks, so we had no way of knowing how long it would take us to reduce them to ashes, or how slow and smelly the whole business would turn out to be. Nor could we have imagined the almost ineradicable marks they'd leave behind them in the grass.

Stella went back to Kenya in September, but we were still burning sacks of prayerbooks in the back yard, off and on, until the end of October. I remember that, because someone suggested we should give the last two sackfuls to the youngsters in Keogh Square who were collecting for their Hallowe'en bonfire. But either we weren't ready to go that public yet – someone said that the parish priest mightn't appreciate it – or we didn't want to give the kids stuff we knew would quench their bonfire rather than brighten it.

We soldiered on and burned the last of Stella's prayerbooks during the first week in November. By then the sides of the barrel had collapsed from fire and rain and rust. And the round base – a circle of dark, smelly, mouldy, bituminous stuff – was burned into the ground about a half-foot deep. It was next to impossible to dig it out, so we just shovelled a layer of earth over it and buried it.

By the time Stella came home next, independence had come to East Africa, and she was full of hope and excitement about Kenya's Uhuru. She told us that she and her friends were thinking of taking up the new government's invitation to become citizens of the young republic, but they decided against that in the end.

This time she was collecting library books, though on a more discriminating basis. She had practical experience now of what Kenyan schoolchildren needed and was more realistic about the quality and quantity of what she intended to take back with her. I don't think there was any need for a bonfire of the books when she left Ireland for Mbooni that time.

She lent me Teilhard de Chardin's *Le Milieu Divin* while she was at home in 1962 and it turned out to be one of my good books of the 1960s. Horizons were beginning to open up for us all just then. There was a buzz about life in convents everywhere. The small, enclosed, domestic world of our nineteenth-century communities was beginning to open up to the rhythm of the world outside. Television had arrived in Ireland, and the Second Vatican Council was in progress in Rome.

I lost track of Stella for a few years after that, but I knew she was busy helping to set up secondary schools in Kenya while the community made shift to equip them with help from whatever sources it could find. One was a bush school in Mbooni in the poor, drought-ridden country of the Kamba people, and the other was located in a needy urban area in southern Nairobi. Over the years I had volunteered several times to go out and work in Kenya, but my letters always seemed to get buried in some pending file at central headquarters in Carysfort.

Towards the end of the 1970s I finally got a chance to visit Stella. By then she was regional superior of the mission in Kenya. It was my first visit to a so-called Third World country. I had never before seen the kind of city where the gleaming headquarters of banks, airlines, international hotel chains and prosperous businesses rose sleekly and profitably on the skyline within a stone's throw of the rawest, most hopeless, and apparently most limitless kind of human misery.

That visit to Africa helped to change my life. It added urgency to my long-held determination to throw in my lot in some way with poor people in the underdeveloped world. But by the time I was ready to leave Ireland, South America rather than Africa was the place I had decided to go.

Back in Dublin for my first holiday from Chile in 1992, I met Stella again. We sat in a corner of Bewley's café in Grafton Street comparing notes and catching up on news of friends and projects. When the coffee was served she tasted it with satisfaction and leaned back in her chair. Savouring it slowly like a tea-taster she pronounced that, with a flavour like that, the coffee beans could only have been grown in the Kenyan highlands.

A pity we weren't into wines, I said, and Chile could have offered her palate something even finer. But these were among the more reassuring products of our two countries. Other aspects of life in our very different corners of the world weren't as promising. There was still a long struggle ahead for both countries and their vast surrounding continents, especially for their hundreds of millions of poor people. I smiled when she told me that she had a project this time to help equip a commercial college in Miguta with accounting machines and computers.

That was four years ago. The other day I had trouble with my word-processor, a quirk in a dual-language programme where the Spanish keyboard insisted on giving me an unwanted diagonal stroke where I needed a hyphen in English. While I was figuring out how to get around the problem, I began to wonder what language Stella's computers were programmed to use. I supposed that East African word-processors were long since working with Kiswahili, but I wondered how long it would be before they'd have programmes available in the language of the Kamba people.

And as I thought back over our progress from prayerbooks to computers I felt a stab of nostalgia for Goldenbridge and my youth – and for the wonderfully acrid smell of our bonfire-in-a-barrel on autumn evenings after school. It struck me, then, that when their day was done and the time came for the burning of the computers, it would probably be much more difficult to make a decent bonfire out of them than it had been to make one from the pied prayerbooks.

PERSONALITIES

Probably the most memorable pair in the community in Goldenbridge when I lived there in the 1960s were Jerome and Jarlath. They seemed elderly to me then, but I suppose they were about the same age as I am now, or maybe a little younger. Age is a shifting perspective.

Like many a couple they were so different we wondered how they ever got along together, Jarlath a slow-moving, shrewd, kindly, unflappable Kerrywoman, and Jerome from Roscommon with a soft, fussy and very-flappable core, kind and hard-working but with small fluttery touches in her make-up.

Jerome was the older of the two by some years. She was thought to be well-connected in the community because she had a cousin who was one of the big names in Carysfort. This was Mother Teresita McCormack who was president of the training college and had been running it along strictly Victorian lines ever since she took over the office in 1936. Her hold on the Carysfort presidency was to become so tenacious and legendary as the decades went by that my old friend, Sister Nathy remarked to me on one occasion in the late 1960s, 'Mark my words. We'll wake up some morning and find her down there in the office, propped up behind that big desk, fixed into her coffin...'.

Teresita was two years short of eighty, and had been head of the training college for thirty-two years when failing health at last forced her to retire. She was a woman of considerable influence in the community during those decades, so Jerome's prospects were thought to be good, not least by herself. She had expectations then, great expectations – the possibility of becoming mother superior in a local community or branch-house in some part of Dublin. I don't think it was the PO this time but some anonymous junior source in the community who christened her 'the expectant mother', pointing out that she had a soft spreading figure to go with the part.

When the Town Planner was appointed to the superior general's council and transferred across the canal to work at repaying a long-standing building debt in Mourne Road early in the 1960s, there was some speculation that Jerome might be appointed to replace her as local superior in Goldenbridge. But she didn't get her promotion on that occasion. For a while after this disappointment she was known as the lady-in-waiting.

The newly-appointed Goldenbridge superior happened to be a friend of Jerome's, an old friend of long standing, and her arrival in the community gave rise for a while to an interesting little triangle. One of the ways in which you could spot pairs of friends in convents in those days was by noticing who said their rosaries together walking around the grounds. Jerome and Jarlath nearly always said theirs walking up and down the side-path beside the school with the sinking foundations.

Now, shortly after the new superior, Mother Thomas, arrived, Peter said to me one day, 'Did you notice that Jerome has taken on extra devotions lately? She's saying her prayers at least twice a day.' And sure enough, she was praying with Jarlath, discreetly as always, along the side-path near the school, and then repeating the process all over again, walking up and down the front avenue with Thomas.

Jerome eventually got her long-awaited appointment. She became superior of the convent in Baggot Street, and I remember with real appreciation the hospitality she showed me there a few years later. For incautious speech at a community assembly I had been relegated from the Carysfort college staff where I had by then been appointed as a junior lecturer under the ageing Teresita. I was now sent off to take charge of a small, struggling school with few pupils and a sizeable building-debt in Rush, in north County Dublin. It was the summer of 1969.

But I badly needed a billet near the university for another six weeks or so to finish my work for the MA, and although I had been relegated from Carysfort with the consent of her powerful cousin, Jerome gave me a warm welcome in Baggot Street. I passed several very agreeable weeks there in the late summer of 1969, studying and taking evening walks in congenial company along the banks of the Grand Canal. A favourite spot was the seat that Patrick Kavanagh had consecrated a few years years earlier with one of his canal-bank sonnets.

When I went back to Goldenbridge for a visit during my holidays from Chile in the summer of 1995, the only two members of the community who were still there and had been in the same community all those years from the time I started out as a black novice in 1959 – they had in fact been there for some years before my arrival – were Jarlath and Fabian. Jarlath´s old friend Jerome was dead these many years, and most of her contemporaries were gone too. Even the PO – who in the end had surprised us all, and herself too maybe, by setting off after her retirement to work in the Cajun country among the bayous of the Mississippi near New Orleans – was dead by then. I stood for a long and meditative moment at her grave by the canal.

Although Jarlath was by now a very old lady, slow, stooped, and wandering at moments, there was still a palpable continuity with the kindly, canny Kerrywoman I had known when I was young. A helpful, practical Sister of Mercy, hard-working and generous, very much in the mould of the old Goldenbridge nuns, she's one of the last of them.

Apart from teaching Infant Boys for nearly fifty years, Jarlath's other lifelong commitment was to the convent social service centre, the side of it that provided clothes at nominal cost for poor families. How many thousands of times she had trooped up and down the stairs to her stores over those fifty years only God could tell.

And in those abundantly-stocked stores of hers – which tended to overflow and occupy all the available space and some space that was not officially available – she kept every kind of item from First Communion clothes to blankets, sheets, bedspreads, curtains, bright little children's outfits for Christmas, shoes, socks, summer dresses, ribbons, purses, hair-slides...

And the buying in of all those items, the measuring of waists, skirt-lengths, trouser-widths and growing feet.... And the patience, the good humour, the Kerry plámás with which she could always get round you to do her, or one of her clients, a favour.... And the people she visited in homes and hospitals.... And the little surprises she always found for the children....

I forgot to inquire if she still had her old headquarters in Castel Gandolfo. This was the community's name for the most famous of her many, and mostly infamous, stores. She had a habit – which invariably annoyed the superior of the house intensely – of letting her goods spill over into any room she found vacant in the convent, upstairs or down. She had been allotted one official store, and it was said that she spent more time there than the Pope spent in his residence in Castel Gandolfo...

I don't suppose anyone in Goldenbridge has inherited Jarlath's mantle. West Dublin, being more prosperous now, probably has no need of such services. But when she goes to join Jerome and her other old friends in the cemetery by the canal, an era in the life of Inchicore and of Ireland will have come to an end, an era in which she played a faithful and generous part.

Fabian, who worked for upwards of forty years in the orphanage in Goldenbridge and oversaw its development from an overcrowded industrial school into a set of well-appointed children's homes with trained staff, was also in the community when I revisited it in 1995. She had no idea then, nor had the rest of the community I think, of the storm of adverse criticism that was to break over the community in the spring of 1996.

Of the twenty-three sisters in the community when I arrived in Goldenbridge in 1959, three were Mayo women. I made a fourth. The oldest was Athanasius, she of the greenhouses and chrysanthemums and the high-windowed chapel-classroom full of Infant Boys. She had the reputation of being a gruff, forthright, eloquent and somewhat fiery woman. She was all that and more besides.

I think she was the one with whom a former member of the community had a vehement difference of opinion one day, over the washtub in the refectory while they were drying the dishes. So opposed were the positions taken up on either side that the other party felt she could only make her point by throwing the greasy suds from the tub over Athens's newly-starched guimp...

That other sister decided to leave the convent shortly afterwards, but not before bequeathing us a quotable phrase and firing a nice Parthian shot over her departing shoulder. When somebody asked her if she was thinking of getting married, she replied without hestitation, 'Certainly not. I have no intention of exchanging one form of bondage for another.'

You couldn't live long in Goldenbridge without appreciating the blunt, kindly, hard-working, good-natured qualities of Athens. She'd often urge me to eat up my food because I was looking too pale and 'dawny'. Not, she added, that it was the pallor of sanctity. That, in Athens' view, was the prerogative of another Mayo woman, Sister Teresa Agnes.

Teasie, as we called her familiarly – though never to her face – was from Knock. A pale, devout, serious and very hard-working woman, she never joined in our animadversions against the PO or the Town Planner. In fact she was a woman in whose presence your levity felt unconsciously rebuked. I sometimes thought that was because she had a very literal mind.

She taught Irish and Religious Studies in the secondary school and brought to her subjects the same serious thoroughness she applied to every other aspect of life. She took her spiritual life extremely seriously and tried to be rigorously fair and honourable in all her dealings. But there was an implacable quality in her. I respected her, but felt that her human register was too restricted to serve me as any kind of useful model.

I was happily surprised many years later when she started writing to me during my first lonely months in Chile. I discovered a humanity there that as a youngster I hadn't given her credit for.

The third of our Mayo women was Xaveria who was in charge of the industrial school during my first few years in Goldenbridge. I remember her as a woman so overworked she hardly seemed to have time to stop and draw her breath, much less to sit down and relax with the rest of us in the community. In personality she was a whirlwind of energy, active, forceful, hard-working, full of vigour and resourcefulness, quick-thinking, fast-moving, and at times so rapid in her speech as to be hard to keep up with – and she was always, always busy.

Because of her long hours of work – a regular day's teaching in school and an almost round-the-clock horarium of duties with the children in the mornings and evenings – I didn't get to know herself or Fabian (her junior on the staff at the time) as well as I knew the other sisters in the community. They lived in the industrial school and had little or no free time to join the rest of the community in the convent even for meals.

I don't think Xaveria would have been easy to get to know closely in any event. I used to think afterwards she was probably so busy during most of her working life she hadn't even time to get to know herself. Being in charge of a big industrial school in those days was a matter of virtually round-the-clock, seven-days-a-week responsibility.

In Goldenbridge it meant running a large house with about 120 children living in it all the year round – ranging from babies to Leaving Cert students. It meant buying shoes and clothes – or having clothes made since there were no Dunnes Stores or Penneys in Dublin at the time; stocking in food and seeing to the cooking of it; seeing that clothes were laundered and sorted (think of 120 pairs of socks, for a start...); seeing to it that there were meals on the table for everybody; taking youngsters to the doctor, the hospital, the dentist; raising funds to build new and more attractive living-quarters for the children; organising a home in the country where they could go in relays for their summer holidays; managing the scarce monies provided by the state for the maintenance of youngsters 'committed' to Goldenbridge by the courts... and the hundred-and-one other things that any head of a household has to be responsible for from day to day.

She didn't have to do it all by herself, of course. But funding and staffing were so meagre, personnel so poorly paid, training for child-care work in Ireland unknown or just acquired on the job, psychological and other support services and structures as yet hardly on the horizon... she had to do, or be responsible for, a very great deal of it herself. I remember going to the Dublin Corporation Market with her one Saturday morning and being astonished at the quantities of food she was buying. It had never struck me before how much it took to feed a 120 children just for one week.

At that stage in my life I was inclined to be in awe of Xaveria. She was so fast-moving, so no-nonsense, so full of a rapid executive energy, you felt instinctively you wouldn't like to make unnecessary problems or waste her time. She was a kind of a natural force, busy doing half-a-dozen things together. So if you wilfully added to the pressures on the already over-stretched domestic system, or caused unnecessary hassle, defiance, or disturbance about the place, it wasn't likely to go unnoticed. On the other hand, if you needed a favour – help, money, a practical service, or to be bailed out of some difficulty a few hours later – if she had it in her power she'd certainly give it to you, and with a good heart.

But those kinds of situation didn't come up much for me. I lived within the same community but worked in what was, in effect, a different world. The poor children I met came mostly from Keogh Square, and many of them appeared to me, at the time, to be in some ways worse off than the children in the orphanage. The level of casual violence some of them suffered was a thing that, in my youth and inexperience, I hadn't even suspected existed before.

Back those days Xaveria didn't seem to me to be a woman who needed sympathy, or would have time to stop and take it if you had offered it to her. But I remember that I sometimes pitied her in the mornings when I saw her nodding off heavily to sleep during the 6.00 a.m. meditation in the chapel. Even she had to rise and show the flag at 5.30, although she might have been up the night before with a sick child, or dealing with a row or a problem among her many young and sometimes seriously-disturbed charges.

The Second Vatican Council hadn't yet arrived to introduce a modicum of common sense into the rigid, monastic horarium of our religious life. And the psychological and other support services that might have helped to deal with the problems of disturbed children - and ensured that too many of them were not committed to care in any one institution - were still several years away in the future.

A quiet Kilkenny woman called Malachy was another contemporary of mine in Goldenbridge. A courteous, conscientious and prayerful woman, she moved around the school almost without your noticing her. She went on afterwards to teach in Rush and then, for many years, in

Arklow. I had to replace her in Goldenbridge as a cookery teacher for a year. This was one of the PO's less inspired improvisations. There were regular burnt offerings in the bin in the cookery kitchen that year.

I remember the note Malachy sent me from Rush the first Christmas after she left Goldenbridge telling me about teaching history to Third Year students in the secondary school. The last item in her letter was the one that stayed in my mind. Joan of Arc, she learned in the course of correcting some Christmas tests, 'ended up in a bonfire, burnt to a steak'.

I fetched up in Rush some years later, myself, but I never had the pleasure of teaching history there.

I couldn't say for sure about the others, but during my last few years in Goldenbridge I was happy with my life and enjoyed what I was doing. That was, broadly speaking, two kinds of things; teaching in the secondary school by day, and studying in the university by night.

When I had shown what I believed was a reasonable reluctance to be pitched in at short notice to teach history to Leaving Cert students in 1960, the PO had looked at me as if I were unbelievably stupid. 'It's a privilege,' she said in her most condescending tones, 'to be given the opportunity to teach my girls.' The emphasis fell on the 'my'.

Whoever owned them – and they were a lively, savvy bunch, very capable, given the prevailing 1950s handicaps, of owning themselves – it was a privilege to teach them, and it was often good craic too. Some of them were among the brightest I ever met in any classroom. And some of those very bright ones had to leave school, for economic reasons, as soon as they did their Inter Cert.

I met some youngsters from the orphanage while I was working in the secondary school in Goldenbridge too. Those who were bright enough got the chance to stay on and study for their Leaving Cert. It was an opportunity that most Irish children didn't have at the time.

The students who came from the industrial school didn't seem to me to be very different from the others. At least I don´t remember them standing out in class in any particular way. Which means, I suppose, that being adolescents, they were insecure, vulnerable and emotionally needy, and probably felt far more lost and lonely than the others around them at times. But how could we attend to the individual needs and sensitivities of each student in the conditions we worked in then?

Trying to get a large class through the Intermediate or Leaving Cert programme in two years – that was the time allotted for schools like Goldenbridge at the time – I doubt if the kind of teaching I did took much account of the individual personalities and sensitivities of the students in front of me. My first pre-Inter Cert class had fifty-seven pupils in it. I was at the beginning of my teaching career too and I had a great deal to learn, especially on the human side.

I'd probably have fitted into the same category as Queen Elizabeth I in an answer that turned up once in a junior history test. Asked what Elizabeth did to spread the Protestant Reformation in Ireland in the sixteenth century, a student replied briefly – though not altogether inaccurately – 'She done her best.' That's probably what I was at too.

I was the fourth of the Mayo women in the Goldenbridge community in 1960. It was an accident of geography that didn't escape the notice of my Leaving Cert history students. They told me at the end of the year that one of the things they liked about me was my 'lovely culchie accent'. Ah, to have been able to keep my big Mayo mouth shut...

THE GROVES OF ACADEME

In 1962 I added a couple of small notches to my personal tally-stick. In May I became a fully-professed member of the Sisters of Mercy. And soon afterwards, in recognition of three years spent among the scholars and squalors of Earlsfort Terrace, the National University of Ireland awarded me a BA degree.

As a night student you couldn't take a degree at honours level in those years. But on the basis of my results I had the option of attending for a further year and reading an honours course which would qualify me for admission to an MA programme in English or Irish or History. It was a toss-up beween English and History, and I found it hard to decide. After an encouraging interview with Professor Dudley Edwards I decided to take History.

I've always resisted the notion that I'm impulsive, which no doubt means that I am. On the way out of Dudley's office - with a warm glow of commitment to Clio and the professor in my heart - I met a neighbour from Inchicore. She was a girl called Avis whom I barely knew up to then. The only thing I knew about her was that she had a passion for Ibsen and for Grand Opera, both areas new and exotic to me at the time. She was going to do English. Why wouldn't I join her, she asked.

To this day I can't be sure why I went along with her to the English Department and signed up for the course. All I can say is that I never regretted it. And I didn't even have to rationalise my choice with the thought that literature is, after all, the more readable part of history. I doubt if I knew then that Albert Camus had said, 'History explains neither the natural universe which came before it, nor the beauty which stands above it.' Although English literature didn't explain these things either, it seemed to stand in a more contemplative and, on the whole, appreciative relationship to them.

I started the English course at the beginning of the college year 1962/63. Ploughing through unfamiliar word-paradigms in an Anglo-Saxon primer bothered me for a while. But when I got as far as reading texts like *The Wanderer*, *The Seafarer*, *The Battle of Maldon*, and *Beowulf*, I knew it was worthwhile. Those darkly elegiac poems about courage and pain, loneliness and heroism, nature and transience were fragments from a world that I seemed to know, although I realised it wasn't to be found on a geographical plane any longer. From Old English I moved on to Langland and Chaucer and, in due course, arrived at a literary landscape that was more familiar to me. I had a good year.

Study – or maybe just the contentment of feeling a good book between my fingers – has always been food and drink to me. Reading English that year gave me more daytime hours in UCD, a lighter teaching load than I had been used to in Goldenbridge, and more free time to study. The year flew.

At four o'clock I'd finish school, have a quick cup of tea and then sprint across Keogh Square, my shortcut, to catch the No. 20 bus on Bulfin Road. I did that so often I had time to take stock of the behaviour of bus crews – the ones who waited the extra half-minute for a panting passenger to make it to the terminal, and the ones who didn't. And then there were the drivers who waited for the children coming out from school to race and catch an early bus home, and the ones who didn't want the bother – and moved off a little ahead of schedule to avoid it.

There were two little girls from Dolphin's Barn attending the primary school in Goldenbridge that year. One was Betty, and I can't remember the name of the other. I could easily have acquired a pleasantly demotic Dublin mutation of my

Mayo accent just by listening to them and chatting with them on the bus. Betty was pronounced 'Behy', a hat was a 'hah', and once or twice we spotted a dog with 'a real scuhy tail,' before the bus dropped them off at 'Fahima' Mansions and me at the 'Universihy'.

Irish universities in the early 1960s had more African students than at any other time I can remember. They were part of the hopeful young cadres from the newly-independent states who were being educated during those years in the universities of the developed world. Some of the young African men had charm and what we were then beginning to call charisma. The women tended to have a shy, timid grace. They didn't find UCD an easy place in which to study.

The first East African women to join the Mercy community in Dublin came to the Carysfort novitiate about that time too. I'd meet Irene, who was Kenyan-born though of a Goan family, in the basement café in UCD once in a while. Over our pale portions of boiled mutton fringed with yellowy fat, and servings of brownish-grey cabbage, she'd describe to me with great nostalgia the culinary delights of her mother's kitchen, all of them apparently piquant, spicy, full of fragrance and colour. No wonder I wanted to go to Africa... or somewhere.

With our long black habits acting as a kind of mobile cloister, our level of participation in the social and cultural life of the university was practically nil. Not for us the Ags' or Engineers' Hops in the Aula Max, or the anti-imperialist Céilís of the politically-minded in Kevin Street. We didn't even get to hear our future government ministers oiling their eloquence at the cumann meetings in the Kevin Barry Room. I didn't lose any sleep over that. But I'd have liked, once in a while, to attend the Literary and Historical Society debates on Saturday nights in the Physics Theatre. They had the reputation of being lively.

Denis Donoghue rebuked us one day in his English class

for the tameness and intellectual lethargy that had overtaken UCD in our time. Nothing of note had happened about the place, he suggested, since James Joyce launched Stephen Daedalus to fame from the steps of the old Royal University on Saint Stephen's Green. We felt agreeably chastened. It was something to think about while you ate your sandwich under the unlagged pipes in the Nuns' Room. There were people who envied us that room too. The pipes meant it was warm in winter.

My sister Sarah was studying history - the course known as Group 8 or, more familiarly, History and History – during some of the years when I was commuting from Goldenbridge to UCD. She was staying at Muckross Hall in Donnybrook. In 1965 she was to take all that history off to central Africa with her. I don't know how it or the memory of Professor Dudley Edwards' special charisma served her during her thirty-one years in Uganda.

She was to find the raw materials of history all around her there – and too close for comfort on several occasions. This was especially true during Idi Amin's eight years in power, which seemed to her and to those who worked with her at the time like a terrifying and barbaric eternity. She was interned near the Tanzanian border during the bloody struggle that eventually put an end to Amin's regime.

1963 seemed to pass even more quickly for me than the years before it. And I don't think it was just for me that those days of the early sixties would turn out to be unforgettable. It was the era of the Beatles, and of Camelot, of young people in California beginning to take to the road, make LSD trips and wear flowers in their hair. 1963 was the year when, for the first time, an American President visited Ireland. It was also the last year of the reign of good Pope John in Rome. And then, in a dark November, it was the year when President John F. Kennedy was shot dead in Dallas.

By that time I was beginning to pick up signals that I might soon have to move on from Goldenbridge. The first indication came when I was told to drop English and enrol for the Higher Diploma in Education. After the rich meadowlands of English literature, the HDip course was nothing but féar gortach.

I developed a kind of resistance to the definitions and theories we were being served up, phrase by phrase, as we tried to keep from nodding off to sleep on the overcrowded benches of the Physics Theatre. And I felt how little the whole thing really amounted to when I – a very indifferently-motivated education student – came first in the class at the end of the year.

After that I was tempted to burn my education books. I didn't, of course, because I had to pass them on to whoever was next in line to do the HDip in the community. Among the ironies of my later life would be the circumstance that I would work as a lecturer in the history of education for a year or two, and later still I'd be appointed president of a college of education. It would be a presidency to end all that college's curious presidencies, but that chapter belongs to a different story.

MOVING ON

The relationship between a branch house like Goldenbridge and the community's central headquarters in Carysfort was interesting in its way. In the 1950s it was a matter of fairly rigid control – especially financial control – by the head-house over the subordinate one, a system which held good until the end of the 1960s. Devolution of decision-making and budgeting to local communities came only in the early 1970s after the reforms of the Second Vatican Council. Before that all the important decisions, especially those involving personnel and money, were taken in Carysfort

He who pays the piper calls the tune. But not everybody is obliged to like the melody that follows. Branch convents were disposed, almost by instinct, to be critical of the tunes called by Carysfort, and as junior members of the community in Goldenbridge we tended to pick up the local attitudes.

I think the relationship between Goldenbridge and Carysfort in those years must have been a bit like that of a small soviet in some remote province, of Azerbaijan say, to the Supreme Soviet in Moscow. You could send a delegate to the General Chapter that elected a Superior General every six years, and if you proved a capable, conforming and hard-working branch member, they might notice you and promote you to be a local councillor or superior.

They might even recruit you eventually to serve in some capacity on the apparatus at central headquarters, but that didn't tend to happen much to people in trench-sectors like Goldenbridge. So while you were there you could afford to feel a foot-soldier's easy dismissiveness about the bosses and theoreticians behind the desks back at staff headquarters.

That was one reason – though certainly not the only one – why I didn't like it when I heard I was being drafted back to Carysfort in 1964. I wasn't being recruited to the central bureaucracy, just brought in to fill a hole as a junior lecturer and general dogsbody in the education department of the training college. But I had been caustic about Carysfort often enough during my five years in Goldenbridge to feel uncomfortable about abandoning my comrades at the front for such a posting.

This was a command, though, and not a choice. I was later to escape for a few years when, for being too outspoken a delegate at a reforming assembly in 1969, I was posted to a struggling little school beside the sea in Rush. But my release from Carysfort on that occasion lasted only a few years.

In retrospect it seems that from the time I completed my five years in Goldenbridge I was being slowly but inexorably co-opted into the central bureaucracy of the congregation. I had what was thought to be 'a good head for administration', and in later years I had to take it on the jaw when some of my young relatives began to use epithets like the President and the Politburo. A few of them eventually took to calling myself and my three sisters – their parents – the Gang of Four.

A betrayal of the free spirit? Likely enough. But who, when young, is wise enough to set a firm face against the subtle seductions of early access to a little power and responsibility within the organisation? Maybe you can change things, you think. Maybe this sorry scheme of things can be remade a bit nearer to your heart's desire. You have your illusions, the most misleading one being that such things are done from above by the exercise of a reasonable and reflective power....

You have only yourself to blame afterwards when you wake up and find that you're headed in the opposite direction from where you thought you were going. Or when you notice that the experience is doing very little for your heart or mind or spirit – very little that's good at any rate.

But during my final months in Goldenbridge I had no presentiment of such problems. The year was 1964. It was summer, and I was spending my last few weeks in the community in Inchicore. It's no exaggeration to say I felt as if my heart would break leaving it.

I had come to care for the school and enjoy my work in it. I was happy with the students and subjects I was teaching. I had taken to the tradition and atmosphere of the place and learned to live contentedly enough with the small austerities of convent life. I liked the unfussy, practical helpfulness of the place and its openness to those who came to it, day after day, with their needs and misfortunes and small hopeful projects.

I liked the people of Inchicore too. I had come to life and begun to have a new sense of myself working with their teenage children. I had even come to terms with living at close quarters with the PO. We navigated each other's territorial waters now with a respectful, though still vaguely guarded, neutrality.

Some of those who had been in the community when I first came had moved on, the older ones to the cemetery, the younger ones to missions in Africa and the USA, and some to houses elsewhere in Dublin. But, in the way of communities, the gaps were filled, new faces appeared at the table, new energies flowed into the system, something wobbled for a while and then settled down. Life changed, adjusted, and went on. I knew it would do the same when I left.

I suppose it's like your first love – not perfect, but still something you're inclined to hold in your heart as a kind of touchstone and never really forget. I felt that way about Goldenbridge, and I was never to feel quite so deeply about any other community I was assigned to in all the years that followed.

A sense of this is dawning on me – breaking the surface of my consciousness and expressing itself in bouts of private tears and public tearfulness – during the last few last weeks I have left in Inchicore. I play records in the community room, try to read the books I've always said I'd read when I had time.... But I can't concentrate, I make no headway.

When I'm not thinking about the misery of leaving Goldenbridge, I'm imagining how awful it'll be to find myself back in Carysfort. I don't want to go there at all - back behind high granite walls. Back to the training college where the ageing Teresita still rules like the dictators who proliferated in Europe when she first got the headship in 1936. Back to the novitiate house where you're expected to walk a straight line, keep custody of the eyes, observe regular hours of silence, turn up punctually for community meals, eat plain food, pray at time-tabled hours, and give good example.... No wonder I'm feeling reluctant.

I'm in a classic 'stuck' mode. I can only see the future as a past I don't want to go back to, not as a new life that, being fundamentally resilient, I can make for myself even in unpropitious circumstances. I haven't yet arrived at that other bit of operational wisdom which will become part of my kit for facing the changes that are to be a recurrent feature of my life from now on.

This is the belief that if you're assigned to work on the top of a telegraph pole and have no alternative, you can eventually bring yourself to settle there – to such an extent that you may even feel a bit annoyed when they come along after a while and tell you to move off.... That was the kind of applied stoicism you needed in order to stay sane and functional in an active religious community in the Ireland of my youth.

I'd had an interview in the training college earlier that summer and it didn't help me much either. The president, Mother Teresita, was more of an administrator than an educator. She operated on a different plane from the PO. So she didn't come on about the privilege it would be for me to teach her girls. What she said was that she couldn't understand someone who didn't appreciate the good fortune of being offered a permanent and pensionable job.

That word 'permanent' sent my heart plummeting to new

depths. It reminded me straight away of the 3,650 boiled eggs.... When I was a postulant in Carysfort, breakfast every morning, without exception, consisted of tea, brown bread and a boiled egg. I hated boiled eggs with a great fervour, and so did my nearest neighbour at the table, Kathleen.

But there was a problem about those eggs. To eat them with relish was said to be the sign of a good vocation, and to show reluctance the sign of a doubtful one. Besides, in a world where elevenses for novices were unknown, this was the staple food that kept you going, Monday to Saturday, from breakfast at 7.45 until 12.30 when you ate your dinner. The Sunday horarium was different. There were elevenses that day alright, but they consisted of boiled eggs and cold milk... In short, whether you liked eggs or hated them, you had little option but to eat them.

Kathleen and I – too bad for us – happened to hate them. But whereas my strategy is not to think about the unpleasant things of life until you absolutely have to, or until you can do something practical about them, Kathleen has a more upfront approach. She tends to calculate the severity of the sore throat by measuring the length of the giraffe's neck.

So she did some elementary totting up about the eggs for breakfast, and one morning, watching me gag again on mine, she leaned over and whispered, 'Do you realise that ten years from now you'll have eaten 3,650 boiled eggs? That's 7,300 between the two of us....'

Those were the figures that shot into my mind the day Mother Teresita told me how fortunate I was to be getting a job in Carysfort College because the position was permanent and pensionable. All I wanted, at the time, was to go back to Goldenbridge and stay there out of harm's way. In fairness to Mother Teresita, I have to say that the pension has since come in handy. The permanency in Carysfort, on the other hand, proved remarkably illusory, and that was a happy outcome, at least for me.

By the time I left Inchicore that August, even the things I

hadn't much liked about the place were adding to my sense of loneliness. I'd look at the little houses on Tram Terrace and think they were much more to my liking than the company directors' mansions opposite the training college in Avoca Avenue.

I'd look at the black Antler suitcase given me as a goodbye gift by Angela, Carmel and Mai, the lay colleagues I knew best in the secondary school, and I'd feel sorry for myself because I wouldn't be having the craic with them anymore. I'd even look at the old bookcase in the corner of the community room that had been given to the community by one of the crustiest curates ever to say Mass in a convent chapel at 7.00 in the morning, and I'd feel a lump in my throat.

By the time I left Goldenbridge I think even the old barracks in Keogh Square – which I had always wished the ground would open and swallow so as to make room for some decent houses – had acquired a sort of nostalgia-value for me because it wouldn't be part of my familiar landscape any more. I had conveniently forgotten the fear I used to feel crossing it, especially after a deranged man had murdered his mother with a hammer there one December night just after I had begun to use it as a short-cut to the bus-stop....

So, I was in a bad way. I played *Eine Kleine Nachtmusik*, the *New World Symphony*, and Handel's *Messiah* on the record-player until the others got fed up with them, and with me. I even took out my Samuel Johnson and gloomily braced myself to face the worst:

> Yet hope not life from Grief or Danger free,
> Nor think the Doom of Man reversed for thee.

I was into doom that summer, all right.

Maybe that was why - although I was no longer destined for a lectureship in English which I'd have liked, but for one in Education which I didn't – they decided in Carysfort that I should accompany Sister Assisium to Stratford-on-Avon to attend the Shakespeare quarter-centenary celebrations and summer school.

It was good strategy and a memorable experience. A magnificent cycle of Shakespeare's English History Plays was being directed by Peter Hall in the Stratford Memorial Theatre that year. We went to see every one of them, queuing up long hours for tickets, and standing in the back of the theatre when we couldn't get seats. For a while I even forgot my grief about Goldenbridge and went through a belated phase of being star-bedazzled and stage-struck.

But in the watches of the night my gloom would return. I don't think I was easy company for Assisium that summer. But she knew me – she had been my English teacher in Carysfort – and she bore kindly with me. We were brought closer by our shared love of the Bard and our trips through the beautiful Warwickshire countryside where he was born four hundred years earlier.

And then in August I had to pack my old brown suitcase and my good new black one, and take the road to Carysfort.

DUBLIN 8, AGAIN

What happened during my years in Carysfort, then and later, belongs to a different story, one that has no immediate relevance to Goldenbridge. I was to spend nearly twenty years working in the training college altogether, though in periods that didn't run consecutively. The tally would be five in Carysfort, five in Rush, and after that back to Carysfort again for a stretch of fourteen-and-a-bit.

Then, after some vicissitudes, and in the midst of some – which is to say about half-way through the long-drawn-out saga of the closure of Carysfort as a College of Education – I was assigned to live again in Inchicore. The year was 1987. I was still working in Blackrock, driving to my office there every morning until the last cohort of BEd students graduated from the college in 1988. But my days in Carysfort were numbered and my job, like the training college itself, was earmarked for extinction.

So, on a Sunday afternoon early in September 1987, I left Carysfort Park and drove out along the canal again to Inchicore. This time I turned left half-way up Saint Vincent's Street instead of taking the right turn for the convent. My new home was on the opposite side of the street. I was to live in Block 4 of the Dublin Corporation Flats in Saint Michael's Estate, the housing complex that had replaced the old barracks in Keogh Square when these were pulled down by Corporation in the 1970s.

For the first few days I had trouble distinguishing Block 4 from the others around it. All the big eight-storey buildings looked the same to me, until I learned to identify the entrance to No. 85 by reading the graffiti. It was a help to spot, from a distance, a run of bold red lettering across the wall near the stairwell which said that this was 'Pinky's House'. I never made the acquaintance of Pinky, but I got to know Baldy, Ollie, Mattie, Willie, Tommo and several others, all prolific artists in the school of graffiti.

I was to share Flat No. 85 with Jo Kennedy. We had known each other as novices in Carysfort in the 1950s but afterwards lived in different communities. She had spent more than twenty years working in the Child Guidance Clinic in the Mater Hospital, and from there was assigned in the mid-1980s to live and work in Saint Michael's Estate.

By the time I came to join her in the Estate she had initiated a number of imaginative youth and community projects and had assembled a committed team of fellow-workers. I had misgivings about how I might manage in the flats, but I knew it was a stroke of good luck to have been assigned to live with Jo.

From the kitchen window in No. 85, the convent was now a set of old grey buildings on the far side of the road. It was the reverse of the view I had when I first arrived in Goldenbridge in 1959. A couple of new Children's Homes, family-sized, had replaced the old industrial school which had been demolished several years before. These were pleasant, roomy red-brick houses, almost indistinguishable from the others around them in a small new scheme of semi-detached family homes opposite the DOM and close to the bank of the canal.

New primary and secondary schools had also been built to replace the old ones that I had known. The secondary school was being run now by a lay colleague from the 1960s – the Carmel who had been one of the donors of the black Antler suitcase. Like so many dedicated Goldenbridge teachers over the years she had devoted an entire lifetime to the children of the area and made trojan efforts to overcome the problems caused by deprivation and underprivilege for those who continued to be affected by those conditions.

As for myself, I wasn't reading history from textbooks

much any more – I had been through a tough little passage of it at first hand during my last few years in Carysfort. Besides, I had reached that stage in life when you can find that the landscape around you is one of the most interesting texts there is. I'd catch myself reading it almost unconsciously as I walked through Inchicore and Kilmainham.

I was still commuting to Blackrock in the mornings, driving east into the sunrise along the canal at 6.45 a.m., turning south at Mespil Road, and then on through a still-peaceful Dublin 4 to Mass in Donnybrook or Booterstown, and on to work in Carysfort. But at weekends I was walking around the district of Dublin 8. And if I had wanted a lesson in the vanity of human wishes – or the urgencies of time that are made relative by history, or the pathos of transience, or whatever – I could hardly have picked a more densely-freighted grid.

My walks generally began near the Grand Canal. I had pleasant memories of that quiet weedy waterway from my earlier years in Inchicore. I remembered trying to count the swans feeding near the lock at Suir Bridge a few times, and finding it nearly impossible to get past ten or twelve because they kept moving about in the water – which led me to wonder how Yeats managed to count up to an accurate fifty-nine...

I also remembered walking along the canal-bank to the Oblate church for Mass on Sunday mornings, and how we liked going there because a young organist called Gerard Gillen often played at the 10.00 a.m. Mass. He was still in his teens but already a fine organist – which probably explained our preference for the Mass in the Oblates.... as some to church repair/ Not for the doctrine but for the music there.

The canal brought to mind a bit of Dublinese I had heard in Goldenbridge when I was teaching in the national school in 1959, a verb that I was never able to locate in any dictionary afterwards. A little girl gave as her excuse for coming late to school the fact that she had to bring her small sister to the Infants' class, and she was 'slingeing' all the way along the canal. It was pronounced 'slinjin'.

The Grand Canal had been the pride of Ireland's hopeful new waterways and the bearer of its investors' high hopes at the end of the eighteenth century. Its brief moment of glory carried it forward into the early decades of the nineteenth. Catherine McAuley travelled on the Grand Canal during the 1830s to found Convents of Mercy in such places as Tullamore, Birr, Charleville, Limerick and Galway.

That was at a moment in Irish history when every little town in the country wanted a convent - in the same way that they'd later want a co-op, a secondary school, a credit union, an advance factory, a tourist complex, a heritage centre, or the like.... So much was hoped for and so much was invested in the Grand Canal project, and yet it was made virtually redundant as a passenger facility by the introduction of the railways in the 1840s.

The flat where I lived stood on the site of the former Keogh Square, those squalid buildings where I had witnessed so much human misery in the 1950s and 1960s. It was also, of course, where Richmond Barracks had stood. In those grey buildings the leaders of the 1916 rising were imprisoned and court-martialled and heard their death-sentences before they were taken down the road to Kilmainham Gaol to be shot.

For some part of the century before that, these barracks had been a place where Irishmen were trained to go out and fight the wars of empire - in India, South Africa, the Sudan and Egypt. They had died in such far-off places as Kabul, Mafeking and Omdurman as well as on the Somme and in Flanders.

From my window in No. 85, I could also see the Royal Hospital where the wounded veterans of earlier wars, including Wellington's campaigns against Napoleon, had come home to die. And below me in the valley of the Liffey were the dark tree-crowns of Islandbridge Memorial Park where the many thousands of Irishmen who died in the Great War and more recent slaughters, are commemorated.

If I walked along the back road by Old Kilmainham I could see the approximate site of a monastery which had once belonged to a medieval religious order, one of those military-religious brotherhoods whose members fought, or dreamed of fighting, in the crusades against Islam for control of the holy places in Jerusalem.

A bit further on, before reaching what remains of the walls of medieval Dublin, I'd pass some old distillery buildings, and see, off to my right, the chimney-stacks of a busy brewery that, after two hundred years, is still producing profitable quantities of a dark malty brew and exporting it to quench thirsts in places as far away as the south of Chile. That would be the beverage Father Mathew's nineteenth-century temperance followers denounced as 'Guinness's Black Protestant Porter'.

From No. 85 Saint Michael's Estate, I could also see the Wellington monument and the southern slopes of the Phoenix Park banking down almost to the edge of the Liffey. That park would remind me of bygone vice-regal splendours, turn-of-the-century royal visits, a papal visit in 1979, but most of all of the visit of President John Fitzgerald Kennedy a few months before he died in 1963. I had watched his helicopter taking off from there as I sat over my history books in a tiny bedroom in Goldenbridge in the damp early summer of that year.

And if I took the path along the Liffey itself, going west from the Memorial Park, I could see a big new European highway swinging west above me, with travellers' horses grazing the weedy slopes that flanked it. I'd stand there sometimes and watch the activities of the water rats in the river. Some were the original four-footed, long-tailed kind. But there were other water *aficionados* too, the members of rowing clubs who had their pavilions along the river bank at Islandbridge. They raced their slim craft so beautifully - with such precise lifting, flashing and dipping of oars - it was wonderful just to stand and watch them.

After that there were other reminders of history that I could see, or sense, if I continued walking west along the river-bank to the old bridge at Chapelizod – a name carrying echoes from the Celtic legend of the fleeing Tristan and Isolde. A world of history with all its forgotten anguishes, triumphs and endurances stretched out on every side of me. But the Liffey valley itself with its broad curving river, its shadowed waters, its currents and dipping trees seemed so peaceful now, only the hum of traffic on the two roads west reminded me that history was still flashing by, even as I stood there thinking about it.

So, it was September 1987, and I was back in Inchicore. But already, in my heart, I was on my way to Chile, the country I had come to love during the ten months sabbatical leave I spent there in 1984-85. What was I doing back in Dublin 8 then, I´d sometimes ask myself. Learning to live and love and appreciate life, I supposed, and meditating a little on such things as truth and freedom, hope and progress. Because truth has its shadow-side and freedom its failures, and progress certainly produces some deep disappointments.

It was nearly twenty-five yars since I had lived in this part of Dublin before. Saint Michael's Estate where Jo and I shared a flat now was a visible reminder of how things had changed during that period – and how they might have got better. The state had made its contribution. Keogh Square, the old barracks, was gone. New family flats and elderly people's houses were built. What we had always dreamed, when I was young in Goldenbridge, would make all the difference, had now happened. New housing, central heating, lifts, sanitation services, caretaking, hot water on tap... the material conditions for a better way of living and bringing up children.

So what had gone wrong that there was still poverty, crime, school absenteeism, casual violence – of which the children were still so often the victims – drugs, AIDS, joy-riding, chronic joblessness, prison sentences...? Why had one neighbour wryly christened it Saint Michael's Mistake?

I didn't know. All I knew – because Jo and I talked about it for hours at night when she'd come back from her meetings - was that there are some kinds of suffering and human inadequacy that will always recur. And there will always be need for people with the heart to reach out, to listen to the unbearable story, to help someone throw a frail bridge or even find a toe-hold on some more hopeful shore – or just to endure the unendurable until some small thing can be done to change it.

Goldenbridge community, with all its shortcomings and limitations, had done that for nearly a hundred and fifty years. But its day was practically over now.

I could see Jo and her teams breaking new ground, training youth and community outreach-workers, incorporating residents of the Estate into leadership courses and new projects so that they could make the interventions that might change things from within. I admired the people who worked on these teams. It was good to see their commitment, their professionalism, their energy and dedication in spite of the difficult and sometimes dispiriting conditions of their work. By contrast with us when we were young in Goldenbridge, they wouldn't have to live in the rigours of an ascetical community. If they wanted to, they could have a freer, more personally-fulfilling life, and they could enjoy the support of a partner or have a family.

I hoped these new projects, in and around Saint Michael's Estate, would grow and develop. I hoped they might release fresh energy and draw on ampler social resources to create a better way forward and a more hopeful future for the young people of the area. It would be a slow process. But life, like truth, is susceptible of a new mutation every time a living creature is born. Hope lies that way.

PART 2

A VIEW FROM VALPARAISO

LETTERS

One day in Valparaiso in March 1996, about seven years after I left Ireland for Chile, I sat down to write a letter to my friend and former flatmate, Sister Jo Kennedy, who still lives at No. 85 Saint Michael's Estate in Inchicore. She gets this odd kind of letter from me occasionally when I have something on my mind that I want to work out, a problem that I'm trying, with difficulty, to put into perspective for myself.

If you live on the other side of the world and haven't sufficient ease or fluency in your adopted language to make the vagaries of Irish public life intelligible to strangers, a letter is a useful clearing-house for confused thoughts. This one was occasioned by the storm of adverse public criticism that broke over Goldenbridge in the spring of 1996 following a television programme which alleged that children in the industrial school there had been treated in harsh and humiliating ways some forty years earlier. The letter was also about what's called here in Chile – with more emotion than we're used to displaying on the subject in Ireland – *la patria*, the homeland.

But this particular letter seemed to go on and on, and in the end I didn't know whether I was writing to Jo, doing a convoluted reflection on an exacerbated topic, talking to myself, or making an impassioned plea to the Irish people. I never posted it because it ended up being something other than a letter.

It ended up, in fact, with the realisation that I must write these memoirs of Goldenbridge, to try to hold in some kind of critical focus for myself that vanished world of the 1950s and 1960s, the period referred to in the television programme. A few extracts from the the script that started out as a letter, will show readily enough why I came to this decision:

....*I first saw Inchicore and Dublin 8 in 1954 through the eyes of a seventeen-year-old student brought up in the country. I had come from west Mayo and an Atlantic landscape of great, bleak, rugged beauty. This part of west-central Dublin, your part by and large, looked grey and poor to me then.*

'*Brought up first of all in the spectacle of beauty which was my only wealth, I had begun with fullness,' as Albert Camus says of his native Tipasa. I couldn't yet see behind the worn facades of this decayed old cityscape whose beauty was not obvious, and whose poverty in the 1950s was so evident on every side.*

But looking back from the perspective of the 1980s, when I went to live in the same part of the city again, I came to the conclusion that the 1950s, my decade of youth and hope, had not been one of the fortunate moments in history anyway. Not in Ireland: and because of the fears, scarcities and hardships of those post-war years, probably not in many other countries in Europe either.

One of the questions I have never been able to answer for myself – other than the answering you do by living and working – shapes itself in different words and images as the years go by. Is your life a vein of rock or ore that you discover and stick with? Or is it a highway that you build from there to the farthest point accessible to you? Or mightn't it be, in fact, a combination of both these things, the foundations of the second being secured with the materials you mine or quarry from the first – but given its subsequent shape, texture and direction by you?

If we start in an unpropitious time or place, or if we find that our given vein is poor – as happens to people all the time, especially those born into hunger and poverty – mustn't the measure of our human achievement lie less in the reach and splendour of the highway we build, than in the effort we made, given our starting-point and materials, to put something there at all?

Questions like this were in my mind as I walked around Dublin

8 when I went back to live there in 1987 shortly before I left Ireland for Chile. I began, gradually, to see the 1950s in another perspective. I thought of it now as that period in post-independence Ireland when things had reached an economic and social nadir from which they could only begin to rise.

Back then, the country – if Inchicore, Kilmainham, and the stretch of Dublin between the two canals was anything to go by – was still ignoring or passively harbouring the deteriorating remains of a defunct empire, and living with many of the negative and resistant attitudes formed during the struggle against that long-resented domination.

In the 1950s the country was poor. The people who lived in central Dublin were, most of them, poor. The graceful buildings of the Royal Hospital in Kilmainham were decayed and filled with storehouse clutter. The Luytens Memorial Park in Islandbridge, built to commemorate the Irishmen who died in the First World War, had been allowed to sink into ruin and neglect. Kilmainham Gaol, high on its escarpment, was an unroofed grey shell. Richmond Barracks housed the squalor of Keogh Square. The South Dublin Union was still, in effect, the Poor House, though it was called Saint Kevin's Hospital.... That was the kind of Dublin 8 that I had come to know in the 1950s.

National independence, it had transpired, wasn't only a question of running up the tricolour and routing the ancient enemy. Freedom and its possibilities and responsibilities were conditions of the mind that we had to grow into, processes we had to learn. A civic pride had to be built up that didn't take its colour from a sense of past wrongs and resentments. That was an old exhausted vein which would run out soon anyway. We had to incorporate our past – all of it, the good and the bad, the native and the foreign – give it its place, and then try to move constructively on.

When the Royal Hospital was refurbished as the Irish Museum of Modern Art, and the Islandbridge Memorial Park was re-dedicated in a fitting condition to those who had died in whatever war, and when Saint James's Hospital emerged from the scatter of gaunt grey buildings that had once been the South Dublin Union (the Sisters of Mercy had worked there too in the hard old Saint Kevin's days when there was no money, do you remember?) then I began to see visible signs of an evolving freedom in Irish civic life....

It seems to me now that such freedom has gradually come into being in what we might call the civic sphere in Ireland but that we haven't yet reached a comparable point of maturity or development with regard to our other crucial inheritance from the past, the matter of religion, faith, spiritual heritage or whatever we choose to call it.

This area, even more than our civic inheritance, has intimately influenced our consciousness and shaped our ways, collective and personal, of responding to life, to ourselves, and to the world around us. Because, for reasons of history and perhaps of national temperament, we had a church long before we had a civitas....

But this is an exacerbated territory. The island that provided one of the last surviving outposts in Europe for the retreating Celts did so among other reasons, we may suppose, because it was congenial in some way to their vision of life. And this vision seemed to have a marked element of the spiritual or religious in it – as well as a pronounced tendency to conflict and bellicosity...

But it is a way of looking at things that is notoriously difficult to hold in clear focus, some would say because the Celts or their learned men, the druids, refused to commit anything of it to record – until the Irish monks formed a religious synthesis between that older Celtic life-view and the literate Christianity that came from Rome in the fifth century...

History seemed to make Ireland's particular Celtic-Christian fusion at first briefly luminous, and then almost endlessly contentious. By the beginning of the nineteenth century, the long-drawn-out conflict between the Protestant and Catholic versions of Christianity in Ireland had reached a point where religion was fused almost inextricably with politics, and, by the third decade of the century, a new phase in Church life was about to begin.

Catholic Emancipation, wrested grudgingly from a reluctant British parliament after a long struggle, created the conditions for *the rise of a new Catholic hegemony on most of the island. But the colour of that hegemony was to be Roman, ultra-montane, and only very-mutedly Celtic...*

It was hardly surprising during the century that followed, when land reform, civic advancement and political independence were denied, deferred and then conceded to the Catholic part of the population with coercion and reservation, that Irish Catholics should assert themselves in the only public sphere they could say was really theirs, the Church. It was even understandable that they should try to do it on their own terms. They had suffered for it, God knows. But it was foolish and short-sighted to attempt to substitute a new religious hegemony for an old one. And it was particularly unwise to proceed by way of a dogmatism in public morality that led to the majority-Church assuming an assertive and high-profile responsibility for the conscience of the nation. In so far as the country's educational services inculcated submission to that dogmatic orthodoxy – and condemned or sanctioned those who failed to comply with it – the seeds of restrictive and resented conformities, which is to say of a felt and fundamental lack of freedom, were being sown.

Irish society is now reaping the whirlwind that was sown during this epoch - a whirlwind of public recrimination and negative criticism. And the erstwhile moral bastions of the society find themselves, inevitably, in the direct line of fire.

'Nothing is fully true which compels us to exclude,' and far too much had been excluded from the well-tended, industriously-kept gardens of Church and society in Ireland, in the late nineteenth and early twentieth centuries. Those who were in charge of those high-walled gardens suffered diminishment because of what was excluded, and the ordinary people who took home the carefully-restricted produce suffered as well. And freedom suffered most of all because it was sharply restricted in some of the most intimate spheres of personal life for those who tried to live by the orthodoxy. This was true for the officers as well as for the foot-soldiers.

And truth was an even more serious casualty – a casualty of outward conformity and double-thinking and the convoluted styles of individual and collective hypocrisy that were widespread because people were afraid to say that what they knew in their hearts and felt in their guts – and, so, could verify from their own experience – was different from what the preached orthodoxy said they should be knowing and thinking and feeling.

The majority Church may have recognised in theory that truth is universal and without boundaries and accessible to all men and women. But its established structures negated that in practice. Truth is as broad as the universe and as unencompassable as a night sky full of stars. It is a universal inheritance around which nobody is entitled to draw boundaries for anyone else. A wise Church, like a wise society, will encourage its members to explore this great, only partially-known and forever expanding universe...

...With my mole's-eye-view I may well have a real corner on the truth. But my truth won't even be a starting-point for the eagle who, they say, can face into the dazzling brightness of the sun.... You can't confine truth to a set of teachings that will fit into one book or one box, just as you can't make a book or a box big enough to fit everybody.... The only kind of box that finally fits everybody is a coffin....

So, truth and freedom were casualties in Irish life in the period following what was, ironically enough, known as Catholic Emancipation. Because freedom of spirit – which needs truth and honesty, courage and openness as its indispensable foundations – must be acquired the hard way. Like civic freedom it must be grown into, nurtured, and encouraged to find its most authentic expressions and allowed to follow courageously its own forms of knowledge and discovery, until it becomes a condition of the individual mind and an enhancement of the shared human experience....

Nothing is finally true that compels us to exclude.... We had excluded far too much. We had confided our conscience, willingly or unwillingly, to the keeping of a civic and religious orthodoxy that operated by framing the 'good' in, and fencing the 'bad' out. But what was excluded in this case was not just the external remains of a fallen empire, but rather some very intimate tracts of our own sensibility, sexuality and spirit.

We had submitted these to the dictates of a public dogmatism which – because some areas of human life are dark, fractious, and difficult to integrate – demanded their renunciation, denial or effective exclusion from the orbit of personal deciding. The last decades of the twentieth century in Ireland have seen a boiling-over of the dark brew that simmered for decades under the lid of this particular cauldron.

...If Irish people are now in the process of reclaiming some fundamental tracts of their common existence for the exercise of personal and social freedom, that can only be a good thing. But is it not possible to advance along this road without the witch hunts, scape-goatings, bitterness and public recriminations – all of them energy-wasting processes – which seem to be endemic in Irish public life of late?

A kindly reading of the current rancours affecting Irish Church life might suggest that the very strength and scope of our older – let's say more inclusive and more nature-oriented – Celtic vision makes us want to punish those who, we may feel, tried to corner, control and effectively displace that vision, or traded it in for a narrow, imported orthodoxy, a dogmatic and diminished thing that set too high a value on external conformity.

A less comforting truth might be that we have taken unto ourselves the judging, condemning and excluding habits - though now clothed in liberal-secular garb - of the narrow offending orthodoxy we're so anxious to be rid of. Whatever the cause, our recent spate of neighbour-baiting does us no credit. And it retards rather than advances our exploration of fresh spiritual territory.

We celebrated Ireland's most recent Nobel Laureate for Literature with great national enthusiasm in 1995, and rightly and happily so. Isn't the time ripe, then, to to attend to the disquiets he has been articulating for us for more than two decades?

> *.... 'What will become of us?'*
> *...........................*
> *I think our very form is bound to change.*
> *Dogs in a siege. Saurian relapses. Pismires.*

Unless forgiveness finds its nerve and voice.
Unless the helmeted and bleeding tree
Can green and open buds like infants' fists
And the fouled magma incubate

Bright nymphs....

The ground we kept our ear to for so long
Is flayed or calloused, and its entrails
Tented by an impious augury.
Our island is full of comfortless noises.'

(Triptych: II Sibyl)

We need, how very urgently we need, to incubate those bright nymphs, or rather to create the conditions favourable for such an incubation. And compassion, forgiveness, tolerance and respect are surely among those conditions. Because genuine freedom – a future with a place for everyone, their crimes, weaknesses, vices and back-slidings notwithstanding – can't be built with the negative materials of blame and rancour and mutual recrimination.

Nor will it be built by a selective and cruel revisionism which tries to make those who walked in improvised moccasins through the undrained swamps of our history, the whipping-boys and scapegoats for our collective failure to be what the more favourable conditions of our own times would allow us to be. Neighbour-baiting and finger-pointing only postpone the day when we examine whatever veins of rock and ore are available to us now, and try to construct a better way forward.

And, if we must look back, surely a sense of fairness towards those who tried and, as we may see it, failed, must make us ask the question: What materials did they have to work with? After centuries of oppression, ignorance and poverty what more free and shining highway could they have built for us with the resources at their disposal? They were making a road out of a swamp, a swamp of hunger and neglect and despair....

Of course they took the materials that came to them from over the sea, or over the Alps or wherever. And they took them on what, to us now, would be unacceptable terms. (We might profitably subject some of our current European orthodoxies to the same kind of scrutiny, and for some of the same reasons....)

The question is, what alternatives did those forebears of ours have? Who was giving them anything except famine conditions and political coercion? And with all their limitations and handicaps, at least they brought us to a point where, if we want to, we can build a different kind of highway into the future.

Secular witch hunts do no more credit to human nature than religious ones. And baiting those whose weaknesses were exacerbated by the hard conditions of their life, holding them up to public odium, or throwing them overboard to the sharks, is not worthy of a free and civilised people. There must be something more generous, more inclusive, more compassionate and comprehensively just that we can call on – maybe from that mythical Celtic heritage of ours – something that will help us to keep the weak on board, bring remedies to their wounds, and sail on with them to what we hope may be a better shore.

Or if we don't have the largeness of spirit for that yet, surely we owe them what even in the Wild West was reckoned to be an elementary kind of justice when the fracas was on in the saloon: 'Don't shoot the piano player, he's doing his best'. There has to be a place in the world and a little kindness for everyone, no matter how badly we think they've played the family piano....

If we have attained a measure of civic freedom in Ireland or are in the process of advancing along that road now, we can surely do the same for our religious inheritance, that is, if we set about it in an intelligent, constructive and reflective way. And it's certainly worth our while to take thought as to what the best way may be. Likewise it's worth reflecting on what we stand to lose if our approach is rejecting, vindictive and careless.

Rejection is a bludgeoning weapon. We may end up injuring some vital and intimate part of ourselves. A Christian Church – particularly one as old and richly-cultured as the Catholic Church – isn't a heritage to be lightly jettisoned by any society, especially if it has been – by ancestral choice and against heavy odds - an integral part of the life of that society for centuries.

Besides it would be bleak to contemplate a future where there was no spiritual community of voluntary association to concern itself with the poor, the inadequate and the weak who lack the means to compete for hope and succour at market prices.

A Church sustains space for reflection, fosters the energy that comes from prayer and beneficent action, transmits a wisdom distilled from long experience, and, as history shows, can perennially tap resources in the human spirit for love, constructiveness, vision, beauty and joy – as well as other things. We can ill afford to destroy an agency that fosters such possibilities, even if religion in its devotional forms is not everybody's cup of tea. The sine qua non of the matter is freedom – a freedom that does not exclude, a freedom based on honesty, truth, openness and respect...

Because if a Church exacts an unacceptable price for the succour it brings to the human spirit – the price of rigid conformity to dogma, say, or the exclusion of some areas of human experience because they are dark and problematic, or the relegation to semi-tolerated status of categories of people who don't fit in with a preconceived ideal of human nature – then it no longer stands in an integral, loving and creative relationship to existing life.... (End of extracts from letter to Jo, dated 11 March 1996.)

I didn't post this letter. Even Jo, my good, loving and patient friend, Jo, might have leaned over gently after the first four or five pages and tipped the script into the bedside drawer and turned on the television. Or maybe she'd just have nodded off to sleep.

Then why didn't I put the letter in the bin myself? I did. That's how this little memoir of Goldenbridge got started – as an effort to give some of these too-abstract thoughts a face, a feeling, a history and perhaps some names.

Before I left for Chile in spring 1989, I went over to Kilmainham Gaol one day to see if the museum there was still exhibiting a very different letter that I remembered from years back. This little note had been framed and kept on display at the entrance to the college library in Carysfort when I was a student there in the 1950s.

It was a letter that Eamon De Valera – for nine years part-time professor of mathematics in the college – had written to the superior of Carysfort explaining why he wouldn't be coming back to work. He had been condemned to death for taking part as a garrison-commander in the Easter Rising in Dublin in 1916. The letter was afterwards donated by the college to Kilmainham Gaol Museum because it was written from a cell in that prison while De Valera was under sentence of death.

It was a short letter, more a note, asking for the community's prayers for his wife and children and saying goodbye until he and the superior, a certain Mother Gonzaga, should 'meet in heaven', as I think he phrased it. At the time, which was April or early May 1916, De Valera had reason to expect that this meeting was imminent. Mother Gonzaga was gravely ill, and he had been sentenced to death. Several of his fellow-leaders of the Rising had already faced the firing squad.

The letter had come to signify different things for me as the years went by. First it was a message from a man under sentence of death. I couldn't even imagine what it was like to have to prepare yourself to stand against a wall and be executed by a firing squad. That he had bothered to write such a note at all under those circumstances impressed me.

Then, of course, in the 1950s de Valera was still a political power in the land. The letter was some sort of link with that familiar and apparently eternal figure. There was also the circumstance that the letter was written to Carysfort, and I was a student in Carysfort. A vicarious connection... they were jejune thoughts.... I was seventeen or eighteen at the time.

Years later, the letter, in so far as I thought about it at all, had changed its significance for me. This was when I learned from Sister Nathy that its intended recipient had never received it. By the time it was delivered to Carysfort Mother Gonzaga was dead.

Soon afterwards De Valera's sentence was commuted to life-imprisonment, a sentence that was wiped out the following year by a prisoners' amnesty. De Valera, it seems, had all kinds of luck, good and bad, and he shared it for as long as he could with the Irish people....

The letter made me think of the thirty-four-year-old maths lecturer and the old nun as having been on a sort of see-saw with death as the plank. Me first, you first, the two of us together...? But fate worked things out differently. Their meeting in heaven, which Dev expected to take place in 1916, was deferred for nearly sixty years, until, after a long life, he died in his bed in 1975. Just as well Mother Gonzaga was peacefully buried in Goldenbridge before she got the letter setting up that date.

When I got to the gaol, Dev's letter wasn't on display. I wandered around for a while in that bare, cold place where some men had faced death, and others had suffered the lingering and anonymous misery of years in prison. Then I walked down towards the Liffey and visited the War Memorial Park.

I sat there for a while near the fountain, among the shades of those other thousands of men who – without the chance, or possibly the literacy, to write a letter at all – had died in the useless hell of the trenches during that same period around 1916. I hoped that some of them at least had the consolation of Tom Kettle's belief that they were dying for a dream born in a herdsman's shed. And for the secret Scripture of the poor.

But I doubted it, because I knew that I was looking at a memorial that spoke not just of lives lost in war, but of a time of abject poverty in Ireland. I suspected that most of these men had died simply because they were poor – and enlisting in the army was at least a job.

You were never far from the occasion for such thoughts if you lived and looked reflectively around you in Dublin 8. What's more they were thoughts you could usefully put in your kit and take away with you to places like Bolivia and Chile.

FROM A VALPARAISO HILL

In September 1989, six months after I left Ireland, I came to live in Valparaiso. I had spent the first two months in a small city in the Bolivian highlands, trying to learn Spanish. That was at the Maryknoll Language Institute in Cochabamba. The rest of the time I survived in a restless, miserable and self-reproachful frame of mind in Santiago where I had hoped I might be able to work in a poor *población*.

During all those months I had been missing the sea. It was one of the lacks in my life during the Goldenbridge years too, but back then the Grand Canal and the Liffey were some kind of substitute for it. So, when I heard of an opening to do voluntary work with a justice organisation in Valparaiso I took the first bus to the coast.

Well, not the first one exactly. The bag with personal documents, money and clothes that I had with me when I got into that bus was robbed in transit. So I had to go back to the *población* in east Santiago and spend several days refurbishing – more identity papers, more money, more clothes – and catch another bus to Valparaiso.

After several months of ups and downs, and a hunt through the city's numerous hills looking for somewhere to live, I finally found a congenial little flat to rent, half-way up the long slopes of Playa Ancha. This is a poor, sprawling, heavily populated hill, criss-crossed by earthquake ravines, and I have a little wooden house – or rather a third-floor flat in the shape of a tiny wooden house – perched on a roof looking out over the Pacific.

There are more than fifty thousand people living in Playa Ancha, a wide southern hilly fringe of the city of Valparaiso. Most of them are poor, many are destitute. The views, however, are magnificent. When I look out my window in the morning what I can see – when everything outside is not wrapped in impenetrable ocean mist – are the roofs and hills of the city, the coastal cordillera, long distant folds of the Andes, the beautiful half-moon bay of Valparaiso and the great restless empty surface of the Pacific.

Beyond that – over the hills and far away to the east – I sometimes imagine I can see Ireland. And like my old friend, Chaucer's Troilus, I fancy I can see my former world now from a new perspective.

Having fallen by the spear of Achilles before the walls of Troy, Troilus was on his way to heaven. En route to the celestial eighth sphere, he looked down at the little orb called earth, and Chaucer tells us:

> As he looked down there came before his eyes
> This little spot of earth, that with the sea
> Lies all embraced, and found he could despise
> This wretched world and hold it vanity
> Measured against the high felicity
> That is in heaven above...

Playa Ancha is anything but a celestial sphere, so I view my former world with less detached feelings than Troilus. What I see and hear of my native country sometimes gladdens me. At other times it makes me feel profoundly sad.

I was sad, for instance, when I heard that, nearly forty years after the alleged events, Goldenbridge Industrial School was portrayed in a televison docu-drama in February 1996, as having ill-treated and humiliated children who lived there in the 1950s. I hoped that the allegations weren't true. Or if they were true in any degree, I hoped that what was portrayed in the programme would turn out to have been, somehow, an exaggeration.

Drama, of its nature, works by isolating and heightening selected events. It seemed probable – indeed it must have been unavoidable – that a brief television programme presenting sad events of the kind that were alleged to have taken place in this case, would have left unexamined many factors of crucial relevance in the context of the time, place and history of the events, as well as the personalities and immediate circumstances in question.

But the pain of a parentless or rejected child is an unfathomable suffering, and I know that Goldenbridge sheltered thousands of such children over the years. I also know that it gave a home to many disturbed and neglected youngsters who weren't necessarily parentless but who had suffered other abuses. To aggravate the misery of such children in any way would have been to increase an already deep and unassuagable pain.

Whether such aggravation was on the scale that injury remembers or collective memory and public accusation embellishes is, in a way, beside the point. In so far as there was harsh treatment or excess in Goldenbridge Industrial School or anywhere else, it was deeply sad for the children, and sad for all of us. It is also particularly sad for the Goldenbridge community because it casts a dark shadow across an otherwise constructive and unselfish record.

These reflections, in the end, moved me to write this book – because I know that Goldenbridge was a good place. It was a busy, caring, struggling, constructive and humanly-compassionate place, even in the hard days of the 1950s when poor people in Ireland suffered painful indignities on all sides. It gave thousands of young people an educational start in life, and its informal social services gave many others a helping hand at difficult points along the way.

And even that part of it that had the hard and thankless job of being an industrial school, gave a home – the best it could manage – to thousands of needy, parentless, abused and abandoned children. That some of them felt pain, unhappiness and subsequent bitterness is sad. But in the hard conditions of those days – and in the impossibility of parenting, simultaneously, more than a hundred children - adverse and painful individual experiences were practically unavoidable, just as they are unavoidable sometimes even in very caring families.

The record will show that Goldenbridge made a constructive contribution to the reform of child-care in Ireland and addressed itself constantly to the improvement of its own children's facilities. If the Irish state's way of providing for needy children in the past was inadequate and penny-pinching and inordinately stressful for those who had to administer it on the ground – and if it is still unsatisfactory – the responsibility for that can hardly be laid at the door of Goldenbridge.

The Children's Homes there still offer facilities to children who need them. And while anyone needs such care – and it is a need that won't go away by just wishing it would – let us hope that in spite of all the hazards that go with such work, someone will go on trying to do it. But let us also hope that they will have more enlightened support and understanding, and better resources from the larger society around them, than has been the case in the past

When Irish society is more mature and free – and less self-lacerating – it may, perhaps, come to appreciate the real contribution made at incalculable personal cost, by communities like Goldenbridge which have seldom figured in the national credit rolls, communities which worked on behalf of the large segment of Irish society that was poor and socially neglected during those long decades. In the meantime, wouldn't the energies we have to spare be better used in fighting poverty wherever it still exists – whether on this side of the world or some other – than in castigating past failures?

Carefully and honestly to establish the facts of a case where something can still be done to redress an old injury is a debt of justice we owe to those who have suffered. But I'm not sure what good it does to go picking over the individual and collective sores of the past to make harrowing headlines and raise a witch hunt that runs the risk of being misdirected and unjust.

The past was harsh and ugly for many precisely because it was poor. And being poor it was subject to the wretchedness and humiliation that flow into people's lives from poverty in any time or place. Poverty is narrowing, demeaning and embittering. Poverty is the enemy that we must still fight, instead of wasting energy criticising the failures of those who were themselves prisoners and victims of a wretched past.

The conviction that we need to fight poverty in all its forms, is probably the most constructive thing we can salvage from the barrage of adverse publicity unloaded on Goldenbridge in the spring of 1996. And if Goldenbridge had to suffer odium – I believe unjust odium – so that we might concentrate on this lesson, the community there shouldn't be disheartened. Their predecessors were in the trenches fighting against poverty since the 1850s. You never get ideal conditions in the trenches.

But we have to wipe out the trenches. And we have to go on believing and struggling and doing our constructive best so that society, some day, will also succeed in wiping out poverty.

DAME FORTUNE'S WHEEL

I went back to Dublin on holidays from Chile in the summer of 1995. It was a glorious summer. I walked from the city-centre to Inchicore along the banks of the Grand Canal on several warm sunny evenings. Young people spilled out from the pubs after work to fill the seats and lie on the grass beside the old towpaths. They drank and made conversation and music where their ancestors had dragged heavy loads. The Temple Bar and Grafton Street were full of youth and summer life. The huge Point Theatre filled and emptied and filled again to receive the stars of the international entertainment circuit, the same ones I might see billed for the big commercial venues in Santiago, Rio and Buenos Aires. And the sparkling, semi-indigenous fare provided by Riverdance filled the same big theatre to capacity night after night.

For me it was a magical summer. I met old friends, spent time with my family, holidayed in a peaceful North of Ireland, walked and shopped in familiar haunts, found old coffee-shops and new bookstores, swam in Dublin Bay and Clew Bay, and enjoyed especially being back for a while in my old base with Jo at No. 85 Saint Michael's Estate.

And yet as I took my walks around the city – the parts I know best, the stretch between Poolbeg lighthouse and Chapelizod, taken as a broad swathe, the hinterland of the Liffey and its two flanking canals – I couldn't help thinking of Valparaiso. Not that the two cities are alike in any social or topographical way. Dublin is a capital city, most of it built on reasonably solid ground. And it has had a millennium of history and culture to shape it. Valparaiso is a provincial seaport of more recent origin, a colonial and commercial place, a small, scattered city rising from a thin strip of reclaimed land and climbing haphazardly over the backs and sides of forty steep, earthquake-riven hills.

The similarity I sensed was more like an intimation, or a sense of admonishment. Dublin is, or seems to be, a prosperous city now. It wasn't always so. It may not always be so. One of the great themes of medieval literature I came across in the days when I took the No. 20 bus from Goldenbridge to Earlsfort Terrace, was the power of Dame Fortune and the unceasing rotations of her wheel – cycles, gyres, or whatever else they're called now by post-modern people.

The medievals took the view that if you were down today, you had every chance of swinging upwards tomorrow. And if you were up, then the only way you could go was down. There was no standing still even though the rich and powerful, being up, generally tried to make the wheel go slow or to stop it altogether. The old Irish proverb-makers had a more succinct way of putting it. They said, Ní huasal ná híseal, ach thuas seal agus thíos seal.

At school in Mayo long ago I learned a poem about Valparaiso. It portrayed the place almost mystically as a cathair bhán faoi'n sléibh / Le h-ais Mara na Síochána. In my imagination I saw a glistening city, a desired place, a magic coastland, a locus of dreams. And so, in many ways, it still is. Its bay and encircling ring of mountains will always be one of nature's great beauties.

A hundred years ago Valparaiso was a bustling seaport, a prosperous commercial and maritime centre, a newly-elegant city enjoying its wealth, culture, and burgeoning good fortune. Artists came to paint it. Poets celebrated it. Foreigners came in large numbers to see it or settle in it. This side of San Francisco it was the most famous of all the Pacific seaports.

But the Panama Canal was cut. The British – those celebrated Valpara-gringos of the city's prosperous era who had lucrative mining and commercial interests in Chile and strong ties with Valparaiso – departed. So did most of the other Europeans. The port declined. The elegant houses fell into decay. Most of the artists and poets took themselves off elsewhere too.

Today nearly half the citizens of Valparaiso live in poverty. The stately houses are crumbling, or somebody is trying to preserve them as heritage pieces on a shoe-string. The hills of the city hide – or display – stark varieties of human misery. In short, it's a place with a briefly-prosperous past, a hand-to-mouth present, and an uncertain future.

Dublin is not like that. Not now. God grant it never will be. But I learned enough history while I was in Goldenbridge and afterwards, to make me have monitory thoughts. European money invested anywhere is a passing phenomenon. It passes when the return on it diminishes or disappears, as it did in Valparaiso and a great many other places around the world. I hope Ireland's current prosperity has a more solid base, and that its fruits will be more widely and justly distributed.

The phase of Irish history when Goldenbridge made its small but dedicated effort on behalf of the West Dublin poor was a time when Fortune's wheel was beginning to swing slowly upwards again for Irish people. Not without travail, and not yet by any means in the style and comfort of the late twentieth century. In fact when Goldenbridge began its work in the 1850s, the country and its capital city were a painfully-long way from prosperity.

Of course we take a less fatalistic view of history than our medieval ancestors. And because we do, it is unwise – and more than a little unjust – to despise the efforts of those who were struggling to make things better for our people in harsher times.

To underestimate the contribution of those who tried to make sure that the poor weren't left totally out of the race, does us no credit either. You don't turn your contempt against someone who gave you a lift when you were tired just because the only vehicle they had was an asscart. If we're wise we don't despise our past either. Its most immediate product is ourselves.

To judge and condemn others by the standards of our own easy life is not just a failure in imagination and largeness of spirit. More radically, it is a failure to understand basic contemporary and historical reality, and it often goes with an unwillingness to notice that millions of people are still struggling today up the same old foothills where our ancestors were trying to find a toe-hold yesterday.

It is not easy – but I don't believe it's impossible – to find a constructive and respectful way of relating to those whose world of poverty we have never had to endure. And for our common humanity's sake it is an effort we must surely make. This applies whether what is involved is our relationship to a historical era of poverty that is now past, or to a contemporary world where poverty still diminishes millions of people's lives even while we enjoy ours.

It is hard, as the Brazilian bishop Helder Camara put it, to keep the soul of a jeep in the body of a Cadillac. But the highway where the Cadillac flashes past didn't spring into existence without the effort, through history, of those who shifted loads on their backs.

To live constructively and respectfully alongside those who are struggling in sub-human conditions now – and they are still hundreds of millions – we don't need to part with our hatchbacks or our Cadillacs. We don't have to feel guilty or wish we could transform the underdeveloped world overnight. But we can almost certainly help someone who really needs it, on this side of the world or the other, in some small, concrete, constructive way.

We can, for example, make it possible for a needy youngster to stay on in school or college for a crucial bit longer, or to train for a job or to find work, or to push forward with a self-help project. We can go part of the way with someone who's trying to make a down payment on a tool-kit, an instrument, or a vehicle they really need – and for many in the world that's still an old van, a bicycle, or even a pushcart.... We can share a hot meal, a cup of coffee, an hour of our time, a letter of recommendation, a word of encouragement, a sympathetic ear.... The possibilities are endless.

That, as I remember it, was the kind of thing they tried to do in Goldenbridge for well over a hundred years. Don't blame them in retrospect that they didn't do it better. Many others didn't do it at all.

EPILOGUE

Two days before I finished this memoir, I went to the cemetery in Playa Ancha with my friend and neighbour Rebecca Perez who was making inquiries about a family plot.

Playa Ancha Cemetery – also called Valparaiso City Cemetery No. 3 – is a wide, uneven, heavily-populated tract of ochre earth sloping down to the edge of the Pacific at the foot of our hill. At its most seaward point, standing on a small headland above yellow cliffs and jagged black rocks, there's a lighthouse which is flanked by a naval school for training light-maintenance personnel. I don't know why, but I think it's picturesque to find a lighthouse beside a cemetery. And a bit ironic too. When you've navigated the worst hazards out there on the ocean, look what's waiting for you back here on land.

Sometimes I make a detour during my walks to the sea in order to pass the cemetery, and now and then, I check to see if the young naval recruits are still polishing the lighthouse windows. Playa Ancha is a famously windy and dusty place. I wish those boys would come up once in a while and polish my windows for me.

As for the cemetery, it has fascinated me from the beginning to see how much life and business thrive around this enclosure for the dead. Undertakers, flower-sellers, monumental sculptors, sellers of railings, pebbles and urns, small boys offering cans of water for your flowers which have already begun to wilt in the hot sun since you bought them, a man ready to supply a ladder if you need to climb to one of the high niches, little roadside stalls under the trees selling cold drinks, ice cream, sandwiches and sweets, drivers of cars and buses waiting for their passengers to return from a burial or a visit to the graves, gate-keepers, groundsmen, guards – this cemetery has recently had some graves desecrated - two harassed-looking officials in a poky office inside the gate and a fairly constant stream of people coming and going to the graves or to make payments or inquiries at the little office.

Cemetery No.3 is a busy place, the exact opposite of my two ancestral churchyards in Louisburgh, those sloping green fields among the West Mayo hills, Kilgeever and Killeen. The opposite also of the two little cemeteries in Goldenbridge that seem to slumber peacefully under a dozing eye of heaven beside the banks of the weedy canal. And yet this busy, overflowing, sun-baked and occasionally earthquaked cemetery in Playa Ancha wouldn't be a bad place to lay your bones.

If you chose a niche on one of the high tiers – which from a distance look, for all the world, like little apartment blocks – you could, if you were still interested in such things, have a fine view of the bay, an evening breeze from the Pacific, and a morning mist most days to cool your increasingly invisible brow. It's a tempting enough location...

While Rebecca was getting short answers and giving a little hassle in return to one of the clerks in the office, I moved off to try and find the community vault of the Cross and Passion Sisters. It's the only place in Valparaiso where I know for certain some Irish people are buried.

I found the vault, a deep, solid, concrete construction like most of the family monuments in that section of the cemetery. Irishwomen as well as English and Chileans – all Passionist sisters who worked in this part of Chile – have been buried here since the early decades of the century. It looks so different, I thought, with its solid railings and locked metal doors, from the Sisters of Mercy cemetery in Goldenbridge where a tiny tablet marks each little rectangle of damp green earth.

When I was small and looked out at the Atlantic from the

shores of Clew Bay, what I loved most was to watch the sun setting beside Clare Island. It sent flakes of golden light dancing like magic scales across the water and made a wonderful glittering path. I might have travelled on that path to get here, I used to think. And I might travel on it again to go elsewhere – to Tierra del Fuego or Chile. Maybe I even came from one of those far-off places to start with?

I never told these thoughts to anyone. A part of me knew they were foolish and fanciful. And yet as I looked out over the Pacific from the cemetery the other day - and realised that I may well be buried here – I knew that my childhood fancies weren't so far-fetched after all. The odd currents that carried me this far and threw me up on the hill of Playa Ancha, having started out in West Mayo, are curious and unexpected too. Maybe our beginnings do know our ends, in some obscure and wishful way.

Before going down to rejoin Rebecca at the gate I read the names of the sisters buried in the vault. And then I thought of Kevin in Goldenbridge who volunteered long ago – when I wasn't particularly keen on the idea – to come back and tell me what it was like on the other side. She kept her promise too though not, of course, in the flesh.

I like the intimations I have about that other side now, in the same way that I like the great empty spaces of the Pacific, a territory where your spirit can wander at will and inscribe its own invisible hieroglyphics on the beautiful, unretentive surface of the water. We are such stuff as dreams are made on, Shakespeare's Prospero tells us. And Yeats adds a more challenging gloss: In dreams begin responsibilities. It's up to us to take it from there.

Playa Ancha, Valparaiso
August 1996